On Teaching Religion

ON TEACHING RELIGION

Essays by

JONATHAN Z. SMITH

Edited by

CHRISTOPHER I. LEHRICH

OXFORD
UNIVERSITY PRESS

OXFORD
UNIVERSITY PRESS

Oxford University Press is a department of the University of Oxford.
It furthers the University's objective of excellence in research, scholarship,
and education by publishing worldwide.

Oxford   New York
Auckland   Cape Town   Dar es Salaam   Hong Kong   Karachi
Kuala Lumpur   Madrid   Melbourne   Mexico City   Nairobi
New Delhi   Shanghai   Taipei   Toronto

With offices in
Argentina   Austria   Brazil   Chile   Czech Republic   France   Greece
Guatemala   Hungary   Italy   Japan   Poland   Portugal   Singapore
South Korea   Switzerland   Thailand   Turkey   Ukraine   Vietnam

Oxford is a registered trademark of Oxford University Press
in the UK and certain other countries.

Published in the United States of America by
Oxford University Press
198 Madison Avenue, New York, NY 10016

Library of Congress Cataloging-in-Publication Data
Smith, Jonathan Z.
On teaching religion : essays by Jonathan Z. Smith / edited by
Christopher I. Lehrich.
p. cm.
Includes index.
ISBN 978-0-19-994429-3 (Hbk.)
ISBN 978-0-19-777701-5 (Pbk.)
1. Religion—Study and teaching.   I. Lehrich, Christopher I.   II. Title.
BL41.S645 2013
200.71—dc23
2012029885

Paperback printed by Marquis Book Printing, Canada

Contents

A Prefatory Note

IN HIS PREFACE to a volume of selected essays, Hugh Kenner gives voice to both the dilemma that bedevils such an undertaking and its partial amelioration: "The essays in this book were without exception commissioned at various times.... But though I have not...altogether chosen my topics, I have chosen what to reprint here."[1] The same applies to the volume at hand.

While I have spoken and written about education since I was a student in high school, most of the essays here collected were commissioned, in the main initially as oral presentations, out of a quite particular conjunction of roles which served to draw attention to the continued musings of a college teacher: the nine years devoted to college administration at the University of Chicago (1973–1982), and my membership on two commissions formed by the Association of American Colleges and Universities that issued two influential national reports on liberal education: *Integrity in the College Curriculum: A Report by the Commission on the Baccalaureate Degree* (1985) and *The Challenge of Connecting Learning: A Project on Liberal Learning and the Arts and Sciences Major* (1990). These efforts, along with more regional and local activities, led to a series of invitations to speak on questions of education and curriculum at some one hundred fifty colleges, universities, professional associations, and regional and national conferences, largely during the years 1973–1990. For some of these, my assignment was quite strictly fashioned, and I would be briefed by the relevant dean or the president of the host institution on the specific, local issues that prompted the invitation. For others, while the general topic was fixed, I was left quite free to develop it in my own fashion. Only a small subset of these seemed of general enough interest to warrant publication at the time.[2] Even fewer seem to me now to merit republication.

In this collection, I have not attempted to update the bibliographical references, to supply more current examples, or to eliminate some repetitions across the various essays. In Kenner's words, "I have chosen what to reprint here," the chief criteria being that each essay seemed still relevant to the contemporary educational scene, that each essay expressed a core of curricular and pedagogical practices that I still subscribe to.

I am grateful for the initiative and the labors of Christopher I. Lehrich which made this publication possible.

Jonathan Z. Smith
June 2012

Notes

1. Hugh Kenner, *Gnomon: Essays on Contemporary Literature* (New York: McDowell, Obolensky, 1958), 5.
2. For a complete list of previous publications, see the appendix to J. Z. Smith, *Relating Religion: Essays in the Study of Religion* (Chicago: University of Chicago Press, 2004), 391–401, cf. ibid., 44 n. 41 for a short-title list of those articles in the appendix focused on education.

On Teaching Religion

Introduction: Approaching the College Classroom

I MEAN MY title in a quite literal sense, especially the verb. What I want to address, this afternoon, is what one needs to be mindful of before beginning to teach a college class.

Forty-four years ago this past September I set out to teach my first class. I had checked out my assigned room the day before. That night I could not sleep. In the early hours of the morning, I rewrote the outline for the opening session, and then reread the initial assignments....

Two weeks ago, I began teaching in our college's social sciences core, a class I have taught each year since 1982.[1] As usual, to my family's thrice-a-year amusement, I had checked out the room the day before (including something I had not known to do that first year, being sure there was chalk for the blackboard). I didn't sleep at all that night, finally getting out of bed, rewriting (twice) the outline for the first session, and rereading the initial assignment.

The process of approaching the college classroom doesn't get any easier...and it shouldn't. It is an awesome responsibility.

A number of years ago I wrote an essay, "The Unknown God: Myth in History," which remains my favorite.[2] In it, I focused on what I termed the "preinterpretative decisions and operations" undertaken by the student of religion prior to exegeting a text. This afternoon, I've taken for my topic the preclassroom "decisions and operations," prior to actually teaching the course. Recognize in advance that not all the "decisions and operations" are yours; they are made within a complex context of institutional and programmatic (or departmental) constraints. Not to speak of a series of student decisions. (I've worried about some of these issues elsewhere; they're not the ones I want to highlight today.)

A first issue is one of time. I find that (no matter how often I've taught a course) it takes me, at a minimum, three to four hours of preparation for every hour in class: each reading assignment needs to be all but memorized; I find it helpful to write out a full set of lecture notes for each class session (even if I don't lecture) as a means of organizing and fixing my thoughts; even if the course is repeated, you can't simply recycle your previous notes—the class will be different in composition, you will revise on the basis of your previous experience. Two courses, each meeting twice, not to speak of reading courses, office hours, advising, staff meetings, committees, schmoozing, and the rest. This means for all practical purposes, one cannot plan or seriously rethink courses during the school year. Therefore, the summer must be reserved not only for any research projects of reading and writing but also for revising or designing courses, along with any reading done as background for those courses. Planning is perforce in advance; the time between quarters, and after grading, is insufficient for aught but tinkering.

Of course you will have to make some decisions even earlier—such as course descriptions which serve as catalog copy, although here one will quickly master the art of being strategically vague. Then too, you will have ordered books at least a term ahead or have decided to use handouts. Either way, you are precommitted to formulations and choices most likely made before or during the summer.

So...what then is your summer's work?

It begins with the terror of a blank page. A terror that is present whether your first, halting attempts to inscribe it are aimed at producing a journal article, a university lecture, or a syllabus for a college class. In each case, you are haunted by what you do not know about your audience. In each case you are troubled by a jumble of thoughts that have to be ordered and refined—at the expense of scrapping a goodly number of them. (If not for reasons of logic and design, then due to strictures of space and time.)

A syllabus is no different than any other mode of academic writing. Follow the rule: "don't start at the beginning; start rather at the end." And throw out nothing you scribble, no matter how ragged or unpromising. (I usually use a loose-leaf notebook with dividers for each class session.) The construction of each course deserves a journal recording the process. Each course, in fact, deserves a journal—a memorial of what worked and didn't; what you expected and what actually occurred; a place to jot revisionary suggestions as the course progresses; to record notes from reading students' course evaluations; a place to preserve your lecture notes along with Xerox copies of sample student papers.

To return to my point: don't start at the beginning, start rather at the end. Even though I haven't given one since I stopped teaching classes with several hundred students, I always begin by trying to imagine a final examination. Not so much the particulars I would want the students to know, but the issues I want them to confront. The skills I want them able to deploy. With this "end" in hand, the blank pages for each class session begin to be filled by possible road maps to move them there. Although the term is associated with secondary education, what in fact you are constructing is a "lesson plan." (I've abstracted a lesson plan for an introductory course to History of Religions that I taught, here, in the early seventies as footnote 33 to the first essay in *Relating Religion*.[3]) This construction is aided by the fact that, over the years, I've worked out a number of issues and skills that I want to focus what goes on in class, regardless of subject matter, and that can be stated as a small set of rules. (You will work out your own—at first, largely reflecting your experiences as students.)

What, above all, I want the students to know is that matters are always more complex than they first appear, and that this is liberating rather than paralyzing. I want them to know that this complexity requires them to make decisions which have consequences.

In the service of this "end," some rules:

1. Students should gain some sense of mastery. Among other things, this means read less rather than more. In principle, the students should have time to read each assignment twice.
2. Always begin with the question of definition, and return to it.
3. Make arguments explicit. Both those found in the readings and those made in class.
4. Nothing must stand alone. Comparison opens space for criticism.[4]
5. A student only knows something well if she can apply it to something else.
6. Students have learned something when they can be reflective about their initial understanding. (This presumes you have built into the course some means of recording initial understandings.)

These goals and rules govern not just the choice of materials to be read but also the strategies of the course. What do I need to do? What will be the mode of instruction? What will the students need to do? What sorts of reading and writing? Recognizing, in advance, that all of this, while finally fixed in the distributed syllabus, is, in fact, less definite than it may

appear due to constraints not entirely in your control, such as the size
and composition of the actual class in contrast to the one you imagined.
(This is one of the thoughts that keeps me awake the night before the
class begins.) An outline of the first class meeting must, therefore, have
default strategies.

Let me illustrate some of these more general reflections with a concrete example: a course I taught for the first time this fall in support of
the Divinity School's collegiate program, which was entitled (not by me),
"Introduction to Religious Studies." (I am concerned, here, with the sorts
of questions you need to raise in thinking through a course—a matter
far more interesting than any given year's particular answers. For this
reason, I have not distributed copies of the syllabus to you.) I hadn't taught
such a course since the early eighties, and so the terror of the blank page
was particularly acute; thinking it through was my sole summer's work.

I began with a set of assumptions about the composition of the class,
including that the majority of students would be potential or enrolled
concentrators in Religious Studies (or the College's Religion and the
Humanities program), and that, therefore, they would be at least second-
or third-year students (and had therefore probably fulfilled most of the
College's core requirements, thus giving me some comparative possibilities to texts in the humanities and social sciences that many of them had
read); that the enrollment would probably be somewhere between twenty
and twenty-eight students. None of these assumptions, in fact, proved correct, and this necessitated some strategic, last-minute revision. I already
knew, from the registrar, before class began, that the class would be larger
(it finally closed at forty-eight). I did not know, until the first day of class,
that less than 10 percent of the students were concentrators in Religious
Studies (there was an equal number of History concentrators), or that a
third of the class would be first-year students. (As this was the fall, that
meant a group of students for whom this was one of their first college
classes.) Because an introduction requires an introducer, I had already
assumed that the class would not have a strict seminar format—but the
numbers made it clear that it would be difficult to hear from every member of the class on a regular basis. The latter is an enduring issue. Even
a relatively small seminar is often taken over by a few vocal individuals,
and you need a countering strategy. When I used to teach large lecture
classes (one hundred or more), I borrowed a tactic from a footnote in an
old Harvard curriculum committee report and reserved five minutes at
the end of each class for the students to write and hand in their answers to

two questions: "What was the most significant thing you learned today?" "What question did you have that was not answered?" The first ten minutes of the next class was devoted to reflecting on their, often surprising, answers to the first question and answering their second. In addition, a rotating set of ten students sat in the first row and served as proxy discussants for the class, talking about the readings with me. In smaller seminars (less than thirty), I usually had two or three students sign up to begin each class discussion with questions and observations about the readings. I had planned on this for "Introduction to Religious Studies," but the numbers made it impracticable. Something different was needed, which required a last-minute revision and retyping of the syllabus: each student was to hand in a set of questions by 10 a.m. each Thursday, which gave me time to incorporate them into the class session at one thirty that afternoon. They were told that these would not be graded, but that their timely submission of these questions would be recorded and might affect their grade. (In a few cases, it did.)

I should add by way of a reminder that class is not the only context for discussion, but that predictability is required, especially office hours that are never cancelled. Alongside these, my students know that I eat lunch in Cobb Hall before class, have coffee in Swift Hall after class, and that they are welcome to join me. But never be distressed if no one comes. Your classes are but one focus of a late adolescent's interests.

The range of students' concentrations, from mathematics and economics to the cluster in history, as well as the group of first-year students, presented less of a problem. It required only particular attention to that first rule of teaching, "Assume nothing; make everything explicit." A word about the latter . . . Students do not have the same questions we have. Their weekly submissions were a forceful reminder of this. Therefore, above all, be explicit about why a question you raise is a question that is important to the field of study.

I shall not review the several hundred pages of notes which record my summer's musing on ways not finally taken in this course. Suffice it to say that enough pages were filled with interrogations of the title that I decided to make this an explicit, early topic of discussion in the class. What was this an introduction to: religion, religions, the study of religion or religions, or religious studies? These are not synonymous. As Gerald Graff (now at Northwestern) persistently reminds us, we need to teach our differences—but I would add, to teach them in such a way that our students have a stake in the question.

One means of accomplishing this is to have them committed to a position early on. Following my second rule, "Always begin with the question of definition, and return to it,"[5] after five minutes of preliminaries the first day, the students were asked to write out definitions of "religion" and the "study of religion." At the beginning of the second session these were handed back, and I spent some time classifying them. These then were compared with a distributed set of definitions from common-usage dictionaries, specialized dictionaries, and brief paragraphs from three theoretical articles reflecting sharply differing approaches (Mel Spiro, Robert Baird's reflections on Tillich, Bruce Lincoln). I should add that one of several suggested final paper topics was an invitation to the students to criticize their initial definitions and to revise them with specific references to readings and class discussions. (More than half the class elected this option.)

This then comprised the first unit of the course. Four sessions devoted to issues and readings arising out of this initial interrogation of the course title. We first read the set of definitions of "religion" already described; then my article "Religion, Religions, Religious" for some historical perspective.[6] For the study of religion, I wanted them to read brief, politically significant, argumentative works, at least one of which would reflect the distinctively American take on the topic. After dozens of discarded choices, I finally settled on the nearly contemporaneous 1960 Marburg declaration of the International Association for the History of Religions and the 1963 Supreme Court decision *Abington v. Schempp*, which was taken (improperly) to legitimate the establishment of departments of religion in public universities.[7]

(I should add that each of the class sessions throughout the quarter began with a list of supplementary readings written on the blackboard with a brief characterization of each. This served two functions: introducing students to names of significant scholars in the field, and signaling the variety of possible approaches to our topic.)

Having done this much reading about religion and the study of religion, it was clear that the remainder of the course (twelve sessions plus a conclusion) needed to be devoted to reading texts from religious traditions. I knew at the outset that I did not want to reify the category of "world religions," and I did not want to teach a survey of a variety of religious ideas.

I will not take time, here, to rehearse the weeks of trying out alternative organizational schema and possible readings for each. I finally settled on two three-week units, one devoted to three types of religion in terms of social formation (religions of traditional peoples, religions of imperial civilizations, religions of voluntary associations—the latter forming most of our students' notions of "religion"). Here, the task was to choose an exemplary instance which would allow the class to read at least one complex text and some briefer materials from the same religious tradition. These were chosen, not just because they exemplified the specific religion and the religious type, but also because they reflected more general issues in religious studies. For example, our first case, the Ngaju Dyak, was chosen not merely because it allowed us to work with the differences between ethnographic and textual studies (an issue which returned in the third unit of the course) but also because, since Indonesian independence, the Dyak had to conform to an Islamic governmental definition of "religion" (thus reprising some of our first week's discussion). The Sumerian king Gudea's lengthy temple-building inscription was the exemplary text for imperial civilizations; 1 Corinthians, for religions of voluntary association.

The third unit of the course (also three weeks) focused on three of the basic elements in religion: myth, ritual, religious specialists. Here the aim was different—a variety of short, cross-cultural readings, in which comparison was one of our explicit aims, and the readings selected to encourage this. For myths, the examples were myths of renewal (to counter the notion that myth is always set in the remote past); for ritual, rites of passage and sacrifice; for religious specialists, priests and shamans. (Among other things, shamanism allowed us to return for a last time to issues of definition, reviewing the extremes ranging from limiting it to circumpolar peoples to New Age expansions.) One of the texts illustrating priesthood, an Ashanti example, was deliberately chosen because it had a number of features in common with shamans, raising both comparative and taxonomic questions. (I was delighted that, in their last set of Thursday morning questions, more than half the students picked up on this and asked about it.)

It will serve no purpose to review all of the decisions as to readings made in the syllabus—this last instance gives you some sense of what sort of rationales led to each choice. Rather, I want to reverse the direction of my title and speak for a moment about "departing a college classroom." There is, of course, grading the students. Something the registrar's office always leaves too little time for. But, more important, perhaps, and in advance of reading the students' course evaluations (which in our college are not available to you until the next quarter), is grading yourself. You will have kept in your journal a set of notes after each class session concerning what worked and did not work, what surprised you, and so forth. You will have made brief revisionary notes after each session on the syllabus. Now that the course is over, you have an opportunity to reflect on the shape of the whole, the relative time spent on topics...a set of notes that will help establish next summer's planning agendum, but that should in no way diminish your sleeplessness before next year's first class meeting.

Notes

The present chapter was previously unpublished. It is a talk to the "Pedagogy and Professionalization Workshop" of the University of Chicago Divinity School, January 13, 2005.—Ed.

1. Referring to the common core at the University of Chicago, on which see also "Re-Forming the Undergraduate Curriculum," 101.—Ed.
2. "The Unknown God: Myth In History," in *Imagining Religion: From Babylon to Jonestown* (Chicago: University of Chicago Press, 1982), 66–89.
3. "When the Chips Are Down," in *Relating Religion: Essays in the Study of Religion* (Chicago: University of Chicago Press, 2004), 39 n. 33. The same material appears, in somewhat more extensive form, in "Basic Problems in the Study of Religion," 24–26.—Ed.
4. On this rule, see also the discussion in "The Introductory Course: Less Is Better," 17–18.—Ed.
5. On the pedagogical centrality of definitions, see "The Introductory Course: Less Is Better," 17; "Scriptures and Histories," 29; and "Re-Forming the Undergraduate Curriculum," 94–95.—Ed.
6. In *Relating Religion*, 179–196.
7. The "Marburg Declaration" was published in *Numen* 7 (1960): 237. *Abington v. Schempp*, 374 U.S. 203 (1963).

PART I

Religion in the Academy

The Introductory Course:
Less Is Better

Better fewer but better.
—V. I. LENIN

IN A SENSE, I prefer the topic I was first invited to speak on: "The Role of Courses in Religion in the Liberal Arts Curriculum...Including an Assessment of the Current State of the Liberal Arts" to the topic I discovered I was expected to speak on when the program arrived in the mail: "How I Would Teach an Introductory Course in Religion." But, no matter. You cannot think about the one without the other. The second topic presupposes the first. That is to say, to think about an introductory course— any introductory course—is to think about the nature of liberal education. The least interesting term in the title is "religion."

I am delighted that such a topic has been proposed. If taken seriously, it marks the beginning of our potential for maturity as a part of the profession of education. Because of this, I note with sadness that this conference is the result of independent entrepreneurship (as was Claude Welch's pioneering work) rather than being a major focus of our putative professional society, the American Academy of Religion [AAR].[1] Note the contrast to a mature discipline such as history which, as early as 1899, had a committee of the American Historical Association [AHA] reporting to a national meeting in plenary session on the teaching of history in secondary schools. In 1905, the same was established for the first year of college work in history. (Both reports, published by the AHA, still merit reading.) In 1967, an important refereed journal, *History Teacher*, was founded. In 1976, the AHA sponsored a major national conference on "The Introductory Course," hotly debated at subsequent annual meetings. In June 1982, the AHA devoted the bulk of its scholarly journal, *The American Historical Review*, to a "forum" on the Western civilization course. A rapid reading of the AHA's annual reports reveals that a significant proportion of presidential addresses have been devoted to issues of education.

I report these matters not entirely by way of invidious comparison, but rather to suggest, on the one hand, how far we have to go as a profession, and, on the other, to signal my delight that you have gathered to take this initial step.

There is nothing necessarily sinister in our lack of an articulate consensus on such matters. We are, after all, in many ways in our infancy. Until the sixties, it would have been almost impossible for anyone doing doctoral work in religious studies to be trained by graduate professors who, themselves, regularly taught undergraduates. I suspect that the majority of present members of the AAR were so trained. In influential fields, such as biblical studies, the pattern persists to this day. That is to say, if graduate education as a whole is notorious for its irresponsible lack of interest in educational issues, in religious studies this is compounded by sheer ignorance. Perhaps this is why our conveners phrased the topic for these evening sessions in the diplomatic subjunctive, "How I would teach..." rather that the reportorial indicative, "How I do teach introductory courses." In my case, I do. It is an activity which is not just indicative but imperative. For almost a decade I have taught nothing but introductory courses in my college. Most are designed for first- and second-year students; no course is designed specifically for majors or, for that matter, for potential majors. In a typical year I teach in the social sciences core, I teach a yearlong sequence in Western civilization, and I teach some sort of introduction to religion. My remarks will be based in part on this experience, in part on my other career. Since 1973, I have worked, spoken, and written as much on liberal education as I have on religion, serving in a variety of administrative roles in the college at Chicago and on national commissions on undergraduate education.

I take as my starting point the proposition that *an introductory course serves the primary function of introducing the student to college-level work*, to work in the liberal arts. Its particular subject matter is of secondary interest (indeed, I suspect it is irrelevant). All of my remarks this evening aim at unpacking this proposition from several vantage points.[2]

First, it is necessary to step back and reflect, briefly, on the nature of the liberal arts curriculum. As I have written elsewhere, as one surveys the more than three thousand institutions of higher learning who, together, offer 534 different kinds of bachelors' degrees, it becomes apparent that there are a multitude of spatial arrangements, the ways in which the blocks of courses are organized: general requirements, major requirements, prerequisites, and the like. Each is appropriate to the peculiar institutions. What remains more or less constant are the temporal arrangements. Whatever we do we must do it in the equivalent of four years. Regardless of the academic calendar, there is almost always less than four full days of teaching time in a *yearlong* course, less than one hundred hours of class meetings. And, there is no reason to presume that any student who takes one course on a given subject will necessarily take another one. Less than one hundred hours may represent, for a significant number of students, at best, their sole course of study in a particular subject matter. It is at this point—with the introductory course—and not with the major that curricular thought must begin. For within such a context, no course can do everything, no course can be complete. The notion of a survey, of "covering," becomes ludicrous under such circumstances. Rather, each course is required to be incomplete, to be self-consciously and articulately selective. We do not celebrate often enough the delicious yet terrifying freedom undergraduate liberal arts education affords the faculty by its rigid temporal constraints. As long as we do not allow ourselves to be misled by that sad heresy that the bachelor's degree is but a preparation for graduate studies (a notion that is becoming pragmatically unjustified; it has never been educationally justifiable), then *there is nothing that must be taught,* there is nothing that cannot be left out. A curriculum, whether represented by a particular course, a program, or a four-year course of study becomes an occasion for deliberate, collegial, institutionalized choice.

I take as a corollary to these observations that each thing taught is taught not because it is "there," but because it connects in some interesting way with something else, because it is an example, an "e.g." of something that is fundamental, something that may serve as a precedent for further acts of interpretation and understanding by providing an arsenal of instances, of paradigmatic events and expressions as resources from which to reason, from which to extend the possibility of intelligibility to that which first appears to be novel or strange. Whether this be perceived as some descriptive notion of the "characteristic," or some more normative notion of the "classical," or some point in-between, matters little. These are issues on which academicians of good will can responsibly disagree.

What ought not to be at controversy is the purpose for which we labor, that long-standing and deeply felt perception of the relationship between liberal learning and citizenship.

I would articulate the grounds of this relationship as follows. From the point of view of the academy, I take it that it is by an act of human will, through language and history, through words and memory, that we are able to fabricate a meaningful world and give place to ourselves. Education comes to life at the moment of tension generated by the double sense of "fabrication," for it means both to build and to lie. For, although we have no other means than language for treating with the world, words are not after all the same as that which they name and describe. Although we have no other recourse but to memory, to precedent, if the world is not forever to be perceived as novel and, hence, remain forever unintelligible, the fit is never exact, nothing is ever quite the same. What is required at this point of tension is the trained capacity for judgment, for appreciating and criticizing the relative adequacy and insufficiency of any proposal of language and memory. What we seek to train in college are individuals who know not only that the world is more complex than it first appears, but also that, therefore, interpretative decisions must be made, decisions of judgment which entail real consequences for which one must take responsibility, from which one may not flee by the dodge of disclaiming expertise. This ultimately political quest for fundamentals, for the acquisition of the powers of informed judgment, for the dual capacities of appreciation and criticism must be the explicit goal of every level of the liberal arts curriculum. The difficult task of making *interpretative decisions* must inform each and every course.

If I were asked to define liberal education while standing on one leg, my answer would be that it is *training in argument about interpretations*. An introductory course, then, is a first step in this training. Arguments and interpretations are what we introduce, our particular subject matter serves merely as the excuse, the occasion, the "e.g."

This may seem a bit airy-fairy to you, so I shall begin again. An introductory course is not best conceived as a first step for future professionals, nor is it best conceived as an occasion for "literacy," for initial acquaintance with some aspects of the "stuff." *An introductory course is concerned primarily with developing the students' capacities for reading, writing, and speaking*—put another way, for interpreting and arguing.[3] This is what they are paying for. This is what we are paid for. We are not as college teachers called upon to display, obsessively, those thorny disciplinary problems internal to the rhetoric of professionals (e.g., in our field, the autonomy and integrity of religious studies). Our trade is educational problems, common (although refracted differently) to all human sciences. So, there are formal tests for an introductory course: it must feature a good deal of *self-conscious* activity in reading, writing, and speaking, because it is not enough that there be required occasions for such activities. In my own courses this means weekly writing assignments on a set theme which requires argumentation. Each piece of writing must be rewritten at least once regardless of grade. Please note: this requires that every piece of writing be returned to the student with useful comments no later than the next class period. In addition, there should be written homework. (Examples: Take pages 21–25 of Durkheim's *Elementary Forms* and reduce his argument to a single paragraph using no words not in Durkheim; or, Here is a list of thirty-three sentences from Louis Dumont, state the point of each in your own words.) At least once a quarter, I call in all students' notebooks and texts. After reading them through, I have individual conferences with each student to go over what they've written and underlined and what this implies as to how they are reading. But this is insufficient. It is not enough that there be all this activity. Both the students and we need help. We need to provide our students with models of good writing. Wherever possible, beyond its intrinsic interest, each text read should be exemplary of good writing and effective argument. We also need to make available to our students the sort of help others provide. For example, in my introductory courses I regularly have the students buy Jack Meiland's little book *College Thinking: How to Get the Best out of College* and discuss portions of it with them.[4]

Even more, we need help. At the most minimal level, most of us do not know how to write a proper writing assignment so as to make clear to the student what is expected of them. Most of us can recognize mistakes in writing and poor argument, we can circle them or write a marginal comment, but most of us do not know how to correct the mistake. We do not know how to help our students improve in the future, how to prevent the problems from recurring. These are not matters where sheer good will or pious wishes help. For example, circling spelling or grammatical errors has been shown, from a pedagogical point of view, to be a waste of time. We need to go to competent professionals and be taught how to teach writing. This is the *basic requirement* for a teacher of introductory courses.

This raises a larger question: the professional responsibilities of college teachers. Bluntly put, *we have as solemn an obligation to "keep up" with the literature and research in education and learning as we do in our particular fields of research.* Even more bluntly, no one should be permitted to teach an introductory course who is not conversant, among other matters, with the literature on the cognitive development of college-age individuals, with issues of critical reasoning and informal logic, and with techniques of writing instruction. While there is some art in teaching, it is, above all, a skilled profession.

To move to the particular question, "How I Teach Introductory Courses in Religion?" I have taught introductory courses in all three modes described by this project: the survey, the comparative, and the disciplinary. From a pedagogical standpoint, there is no difference between them. They all require explicit attention to matters of reading, writing, and speaking, to issues of interpretation and argument—to that most fundamental social goal of liberal education, the bringing of private percept into public, civil discourse. This requires adherence to the pedagogical rule that "less is better." For example, my yearlong survey, "Religion in Western Civilization," is organized around a single, two-part issue: "What is a tradition? How are traditions maintained through acts of reinterpretation?" And three pairs of topics: kingship/cosmology; purity-impurity/wisdom; voluntary associations/salvation. Note that the first member of each pair is preeminently social; the second, ideological. This allows a modest introduction of theoretical issues into a course which consists, essentially, of reading "classic" primary texts.

All three modes require explicit recognition of the educational dilemma of breadth and depth. Each of my introductory courses divides each topic into two parts. The first, usually entitled "the vocabulary of x," features the rapid reading of a wide variety of little snippets simply to get a sense of the semantic range of the topic and to experiment with what clusters of relationships can be discerned within the vocabulary. The second part features the slow and careful reading of a few exemplary documents. Each section of each introductory course is preceded by a lecture in which the topic is introduced but, of more importance, in which the syllabus is "unpacked." The students need to know what decisions I have made and why. What have I included? What have I excluded? They also need to hear some cost accounting of these decisions. That is to say, I want my students to use the syllabus as an occasion for reflection on judgment and consequences, to be conscious of the fact that a syllabus is not self-evident, but (hopefully) a carefully constructed argument.

Beyond these generalities, I have two, and only two, criteria which govern the selection of the examples and the organization of the syllabi: one has more to do with the form, the other with content.

Each of my introductory courses is organized around the notion of argument and the insistence that the building blocks of argument remain constant: definitions, data, classifications, and explanations. If we are reading second-order texts together, we have to learn to recognize these in others; if we are reading primary religious documents, we may have to construct them for ourselves. In some of my introductory courses, we devote the first week to explicit attention to these matters, thereby building a vocabulary by which we can identify and discuss these elements in subsequent readings. In other introductory courses, the courses themselves are organized around these rubrics and we spend the entire term exploring them. For example, any introductory course must begin with the question of definition ("What is civilization?" "What is Western?"—I have my students take out a piece of paper and write their answers to these questions within the first five minutes of the first day of the course. We spend the rest of the period classifying their answers, discussing them, and discussing what makes a good definition); or a unit of a course might be designed to display the question of definition (in one introduction, I use as readings: Penner and Yonan, W. C. Smith, R. Otto, P. Berger, M. Spiro, and R. B. Edwards).[5]

The second rule is more central: *nothing must stand alone.* That is to say, every item studied in an introductory course must have a conversation partner. Items must have, or be made to have, arguments with each other. The possibilities are manifold; the only requirement is that the juxtaposition be interesting. For example, in what you have termed disciplinary courses, I search very hard for readings which contain two representative scholars who employ identical data (e.g., Piddocks vs. Orans, the Kronenfelds vs. Lévi-Strauss); or for a striking juxtaposition which reveals hidden implications in a given position (e.g., showing Leni Riefenstahl's *Triumph of the Will* after reading Durkheim's *Elementary Forms*; reading the classic pornographic novel, *The Story of O* after reading Eliade and others on initiation).

Congruent with a concern for the relationship between the enterprise of liberal education and citizenship and with the observation that critical inquiry as often taught ("there's always another point of view") too frequently results in cynicism, the students must not be left with mere juxtaposition. There must be explicit attention to the possibilities and problems of translating, of reducing, one item in terms of the other. And, there must be explicit attention to consequences and entailments. What if the world really is as so-and-so describes it? What would it mean to live in such a world? What acts of translation must I perform? What would be gained? What would be lost?

Finally, if possible, there should be a "laboratory" component in an introductory course. The students should have to do something which fosters reflection on all of the above. It can be based on observation (for example, in the unit on purity/impurity I have my students describe an actual meal, determine the rules which governed it, and attempt to reduce them to a system. This is in no way the same as the ancient rules, but, it provokes thought). It can be based on a real research (for example, in my Bible and Western Civilization sequence, each student chooses a Bible printed before 1750 from our rare book collection and attempts to determine the significance of the format. The text is in each case the same, but the Bibles look very different. Why?). It can be explicitly argumentative (for example, I have my students write a "tenth" opinion, employing some particular perspective, on some recent Supreme Court decision involving religion after reading the transcript—e.g., What would Durkheim have ruled in the Rhode Island creche case?[6]).

In sum, there is nothing distinctive to the issue of introducing religion. Its problems are indigenous to the genre of introductory courses. The issues are not inherently disciplinary. They are primarily pedagogical. This is as it should be. For our task, in the long run, is not to introduce or teach our field for its own sake, but to use our field in the service of the broader and more fundamental enterprise of liberal learning.

Notes

Mark Juergensmeyer, ed., *Teaching the Introductory Course in Religious Studies: A Sourcebook* (Atlanta: Scholars Press, 1991), 185–192. Reprinted by permission of the American Academy of Religion.

1. On the AAR and the profession of education, see "Connections," 59–60 passim.—Ed.

2. I have taken the next four paragraphs, with minor alterations, from J. Z. Smith, "No Need to Travel to the Indies: Judaism and the Study of Religion," in *Take Judaism, For Example*, ed. Jacob Neusner (Chicago: University of Chicago Press, 1983), 216–217. For another version, see "Why the College Major?" 115–16. [Note that the distinction between high school and college work, the latter seen centrally as "training in argument about interpretations," is central in "Puzzlement," 119–35.—Ed.]

3. On the concern with skills and capacities, see "Re-Forming the Undergraduate Curriculum," 100–102.—Ed.

4. Jack Meiland, *College Thinking: How to Get the Best out of College* (New York: Signet, 1981).
5. On the pedagogical centrality of definitions, see "Approaching the College Classroom," 6; "Scriptures and Histories," 25; and "Re-Forming the Undergraduate Curriculum," 94–95.—Ed.
6. *Lynch v. Donnelly*, 465 U.S. 668 (1984). See also Smith's execution of this assignment: "God Save This Honourable Court," in *Relating Religion*, 375–390.—Ed.

2

Basic Problems in the Study
of Religion

A. Background Information

I have taught versions of this course nine times over a seven-year period, both at the University of California, Santa Barbara, and the University of Chicago. The course is designed as a large-enrollment, lecture course (and would profit, though this is not possible at Chicago, from discussion groups). At present the enrollment is a mixture of undergraduate and graduate students representing a wide variety of disciplines.

There is *no* undergraduate Department of Religion at the University of Chicago, although there is a major graduate program. Rather both the present undergraduate program, Religion and the Humanities, and its predecessor, History and Philosophy of Religion, have had to draw upon the interests and availability of competent faculty in other departments of the University to offer or cross-list courses for college students in religion. The chief problem (addressed in the description of the present program) has been (1) to design a set of "curricular boxes" which could be taught by different faculty from different disciplines each year and (2) to insure that these courses address fundamental issues so that they could be used as a base for interested students to design a program of study (courses in other departments and tutorials) without the overall design or security that a department provides.

I would suggest that the total design of the program is of interest in its attempt to convert what may appear as an organizational vice into an educational virtue. The particular course is an example of an attempt to design an introduction to a fundamental problem in the *study* of religion—in this case the problem of how to read a religious document. I make no special claim for the particular readings, they change each year. Only for the sorts of issues that are addressed by considering them. It would be possible to construct a similar course on the basis of more familiar material (e.g., the Bible) with an analogous set of fundamental problems.

The Program in Religion and the Humanities

The aim of an undergraduate program of studies in religion should be the understanding of religion as one of man's primary responses to and expressions of the human condition. Religion is one of the major means man possesses for constructing a significant world and for establishing his existence by expressing the truth of what it is to be human. The student should be led to an appreciation of religious creativity as a constitutive force in human history, and to the problematics of religion as it negotiates between its traditions and the world in which it finds itself. The student should also be led to an appreciation of the difficult task of a critical, disciplined study of religion.

The undergraduate program in Religion and the Humanities is designed to meet these needs. By locating the program within the Humanities Collegiate Division and by utilizing a number of existing courses drawn from a variety of departments, we affirm our belief that the study of religion is a mode of humane inquiry, that the data of religion (its literature, history, etc.) are not the privileged possession of any single discipline. By proposing a core curriculum of problem-oriented courses, we affirm our belief that there is an intellectual tradition of the study of religion which must be mastered. By this combination of breadth and sharp focus, by exploring religion within its widest cultural context and by reflecting on the act of understanding religion, the program represents a significant departure from the usual models for departments of religious studies. This departure is consonant with the University's long-standing tradition of reflection on fundamental questions and of encouraging interdisciplinary inquiry and research.

The Curriculum: Core Courses

At the heart of this program is a core of four courses which serve as a focus of integration and coherence, and give the student a disciplined base which will allow him to make maximum use of other relevant courses in the College, the Divinity School, and the Graduate Divisions.

The four courses, open to any student in the College, are described as follows:[1]

1. Basic Problems in the Study of Religion

The intent would be to isolate a key problem in the study of religion and critically examine a representative sample of the kinds of data which give rise to the problem and the sorts of answers which have been proposed. For example, such a course might test the adequacy of traditional definitions of religion or criteria for religious authenticity by examining several of the "new religions" which have arisen in the last century. Or, the course might examine a number of scholars who distinguish sharply between primitive and modern or Eastern and Western thought and assess the grounds and utility of such dichotomies.

2. Basic Structures in the Interpretation of Religion

Recognizing that there is no single method adequate to the interpretation of religious phenomena, this course would ask the professor to stipulate an approach (e.g., a functionalist, psychoanalytical, socioeconomic, structural, phenomenological approach) and carry it through a given body of religious material with rigor and with self-criticism.

3. Basic Structures in the Self-Interpretation of Religion

This course would recognize that each religious tradition has developed languages and structures of thought for interpreting itself to its believers and to others who are not members of the tradition. Consequently this course would analyze both internally and externally directed religious documents as structures of creative thought and affirmation. This course might either focus on the strategies and logic of one particular tradition (its theology, ethics) or might venture a comparative theology or ethics and explore how a primitive, Eastern, or Western religious thinker or community interprets their received tradition to their contemporaries and others.

4. Religious Literature and Expression

This course would focus on specific religious texts, examining them in the light of a variety of interpretive techniques. It would examine forms of literature or other modes of expression which are characteristically religious, as they are found either within a single tradition or comparatively (for example: religious architecture, sacred books, liturgies, religious biographies). The course would aim at presenting those exegetical methods developed by modern scholarship as well as taking into account interpretations which are traditional within those religious communities from which the texts have been taken.

The first two courses focus on key methodological problems and as such provide an introduction to the kinds of questions which exercise the student of religion. The second two courses emphasize the characteristic data and problematics of interpretation of religious materials. All four, taken together, serve as both resources and an agenda for the student's further inquiries.

For reasons of both economy and intellectual design, the courses have the character of a series of "curricular boxes." The same sort of course is being offered each year, but not necessarily by the same individual or on the same group of materials. There must be agreement as to the nature of the courses, but not a strict description. This reflects our judgment that (1) there are a set of fundamental questions and skills which concern any student of religion; (2) these questions are not the privileged possession of any one discipline or perspective.

Other Courses in the Program

In addition to these four courses which have been specially designed as the program's core, the student is expected to take at least one Western and one non-Western civilization sequence. The College is fortunate in having a number of yearlong civilizational courses which offer a more varied and extensive treatment of world religions within their historical and cultural contexts than can be found in most undergraduate departments of religion with their separate courses on Christianity, Buddhism, Islam. In these sequences, the student is exposed to a variety of methods and to the problems of interpreting religion within a wider cultural setting.

While the core courses are open to any student in the College, they are designed to constitute the first step in a degree program. After the student has completed the core requirements, he will be expected to concentrate for a significant portion of his remaining work on a particular religious tradition or set of problems utilizing the wide range of College and Graduate courses regularly offered by various departments on some aspect of religion, as well as the possibility for supervised independent study.

The Program, by focusing on fundamental questions in the study of religion, has integrity as a mode of general studies. Through its interdisciplinary character, it will provide a thorough grounding for graduate work in religious studies as well as in adjacent fields of inquiry in the humanities and social sciences.

B. Syllabus for the Course: Basic Problems in the Study of Religion

This course is designed as an introduction to a basic problem in the *study* of religion. We shall focus on the problems of reading and understanding religious texts through the interpretation of specific documents. Using these documents as "take off" points, we shall be concerned with four areas: (a) fundamental structures of religious experience, expression, and behavior; (b) representative cultural patterns of religious experience, expression, and behavior; (c) significant problems and theories in the history of the study of religion; (d) techniques of interpretation.

Requirements

(1) Using the concepts and techniques gained in the course, each student will essay an interpretation (and an agenda of questions for further research) of the three versions of the origin myth of the Medicine rite of the Winnebago as published by Paul Radin, *Indiana University Publications in Anthropology and Linguistics*, Memoir 3 (1950). Reference should also be made to Radin's account in *The Winnebago* (37th Report of the American Bureau of Ethnology—now available as a University of Nebraska Bison Paperback) and *The Road of Life and Death* (New York: Pantheon, 1945).

(2) There will be a final examination. Write an essay on the following quotation from David Maybury-Lewis and indicate how you would go about solving his problem: "If I read a myth, select certain elements from it, and arrange them in a pattern, that structure or pattern is bound to be in the material unless I have misread the text or demonstrably misrendered it. The fact of its being there does not, however, indicate that my arrangement is anything more than my personal whim. A myth is therefore bound to have a number of possible patterns or structures that are both in the material and in the eye of the beholder. The problem is to decide between them and to determine the significance of any of them."[2]

Outline of Course   (I have summarized some of the issues discussed for each reading from my lecture notes.)

Session 1   Introduction: What is a text?

Sessions 2–4   Reading: Alexander Heidel, *The Gilgamesh Epic and Old Testament Parallels* (Chicago: University of Chicago Press, 1946). Introduction to religion of an archaic, urban, agricultural culture; the problems of editing a text when there is no complete text but only fragmentary versions. Question of whether there is an "original text," criteria for its reconstruction. Relation of epic materials to religious traditions. Possibility of pattern: hero, fertility deity, sacred kingship. Problem of assessing parallels: the Atrahasis epic, Genesis flood-story.

Sessions 5–6   Reading: Hare Hongi, trans., "A Maori Cosmogony," *Journal of the Polynesian Society* 16, no. 3 (1907): 113–119. Highly developed "primitive" society. Problem of reconstructing history without written documents (diffusion, migration, etc.). Text is a cosmogonic myth: definition of myth; high god structure. Conditions under which text collected in field. Text is both myth and homily. Myth not naked text but encased in native exegetical tradition. Text is not, in fact, archaic, it is a late forgery containing Maori anti-Christian propaganda. Use of specific historical knowledge in interpreting the intentionality of a given text. Relation of evidence to theory: text is decisive for Eliade-Pettazzoni definition of myth and high god—does the fact that it is not archaic affect their theories?

Sessions 7–8   Reading: Joseph M. Kitagawa, "Ainu Bear Festival (*Iyomante*)," *History of Religions* 1, no. 1 (Summer 1961): 95–151. Archaic hunting culture (relation to paleo-Siberian). Characteristics: hunt as religious activity, shamanism, Master of Animals, sacrifice. Ritual text rather than narrative. Observer's report rather than a primary document (do we interpret differently). Problem of field-work, participant observer. Problem of credibility. Do we believe what we are told?

Sessions 9–12   Readings: "Hainuwele Myth," in Joseph Campbell, *Primitive Mythology* (New York: Penguin, 1969), 173–176; and Ivor H. N. Evans, *The Religion of the Tempasuk Dusuns of North Borneo* (Cambridge: Cambridge

University Press, 1953), 15–17, 372–373. Archaic agricultural materials, Tuber and paleo-Asiatic rice cultures. *Kulturkreis* theory: relation of tuber, coconut,
sago, grain. The structure of dema deity as present
in Hainuwele, compared with other dema texts. Does
pattern fit? Use of myth to reconstruct ritual. Multiple
versions of same myth—how to assess. Introduction to
several folklore theories.

Sessions 13–15   Reading: Kenelm Burridge, *Mambu* (London:
Methuen, 1960), 154–165. Etiology of cargo cult.
Categories of cargo, problem of religious persistence
and change, church/sect, prophet and charisma, initiation. Modern myth still evolving (four collected
versions). As text has best ethnography, detailed interpretation using phenomenological, functional, psychological, and structural approaches.

Sessions 16–20   Reading: *Purushasukta* (Rig Veda X.90). Three texts
in last sessions: Hainuwele, Mambu, and Purusha all
narrate a primordial killing. Different cultures—is
there a pattern? How would it be specified? Tension
between morphology and history. Problem of "canon,"
highly self-conscious literary-religious tradition. Oral-
written. Use of a text both explicitly and implicitly in a
self-conscious tradition. Notion of homology. What is
a tradition? Exploration of parallel Sanskritic texts and
commentaries. Relation of myth to "theology." Use of
text in temple construction, Brahmanic sacrifice, and
yoga.

Final Reflections

There are two final observations which ought to be made, both reflecting
criticisms by students. As I have already indicated, a serious problem is
the lack of small discussion groups. In a course which emphasizes the
problematics of interpretation, University of Chicago policy against the
employment of teaching assistants presents an almost insurmountable
obstacle. We have tried, by fostering informal lunch and evening groups,
to address this situation but the results have not been wholly satisfactory.
Next year, having learned from my colleagues in the society's project, I

will institute a set of mini-courses which will allow discussion with me of either the assigned texts or analogous materials.

The second problem is more fundamental. A number of students have expressed distress that there is no "happy ending." The course emphasizes problems and criticisms of previous work without providing a constructive alternative. A number of colleagues at the regional meetings expressed similar reservations. I can only say that if the course has this effect, it has been successful. I conceive of the role of the college teacher to be precisely that of insuring that his students have "wrinkles on their brows," that they become adept in the "hermeneutics of suspicion." I believe for those students that take no further courses in religious studies, they have learned how to be cold-blooded about humanistic materials; for those students who continue to take other courses in religious studies, the effect of this course will be relativized by other offerings.

Notes

Luke T. Johnson, ed., *Teaching Religion to Undergraduates: Some Approaches and Ideas from Teachers to Teachers* (Society for Religion in Higher Education, 1973), 47–53. Reprinted by permission.

1. Compare this curricular description with that in "Here and Now: Prospects for Graduate Education," 40–45.—Ed.
2. David Maybury-Lewis, review of *Du miel au cendres*, by Claude Lévi-Strauss, *American Anthropologist*, n.s. 71 (1969): 118–119.

3

Scriptures and Histories

I AM DELIGHTED to have this opportunity to participate in celebrating the contributions of Wilfred Cantwell Smith. For there is a sphere of faith and a cumulative tradition which we share: the academy and its work. It has brought us together for conversations, from time to time, which have been memorable for me in experiencing Smith's uncommon generosity and stubborn, unwavering commitment to discourse, punctuated by insights which always reveal new dimensions to familiar objects of thought.

I am also delighted (and relieved) to have the advantage of refracting my appreciation in terms of the subject, "Scriptures and Histories," in advance of Smith's long-awaited book on the subject. At the very least, this leaves me a more open playing field.

From one point of view, Smith and I have relatively little in common. Although I read him, with interest and respect, as each new book comes out, he has not played much of a role in my constructive work. We share last names, but not much else. However, from another vantage point, and one that I value more, Smith's work and general demeanor has been a constant challenge, a source of stimulation, and a model for emulation. I refer here to the teaching enterprise where, largely unknown to Smith, and to anyone else I suppose, he has been a major, imaginary conversation partner for almost thirty years.

The Meaning and End of Religion was the first book of theory I ever taught in its entirety, with my other colleagues, at a senior seminar at Dartmouth College in 1964, the year it appeared in paperback.[1] While much of my own theoretical work has been based on an affirmation of Smith's historical study of the word "religion," it has been based, as well, on an affirmative answer to Smith's rhetorical question, "Is the concept adequate?" That is to say, as I tried to suggest in the opening paragraph of *Imagining Religion*, from my relentlessly anthropological point of view,

I glory in all those understandings of the term that Smith found so troublesome. But this is *not* an argument I wish to rehearse here.

Rather, what I learned most from *Meaning and End of Religion* was the absolute importance of starting any course of study with a history of its vocabulary and reflection on the implications of that history. So seriously did I take this endeavor that, in the years I was associated with the History of Religions field at Chicago, I used to argue for an additional language requirement, alongside of the usual studies of others' languages, a requirement in Christian theology and Enlightenment/post-Enlightenment philosophy, arguing that these, for better or worse (alas, often the latter), provided students with their translation terms whose history and attendant baggage they must not be ignorant of. At any rate, as any of my college students will testify, in every course I teach, the first week or two is devoted to the rationale of the syllabus as an argumentative document, and to a history of terminology, of what Raymond Williams calls, "key words." As any of my college students will also testify, the final assignment is almost always a journal which meditates on and revises their initial definitions in terms of the lexical history learned and the primary and secondary materials studied.[2] But again, this is not the aspect of Smith's work and influence on which I wish to dwell.

As an academic child of the early sixties, those heady days in which a creative misreading of the U.S. Supreme Court's *Schempp* decision made possible the extension of religious studies into the American state university system with its attendant hope, now utterly lost, that a new mode of religious studies was to be born, I have always looked with deepest suspicion on Bible courses. Surely their presence in the curriculum, their privileged place (with, often two appointments committed) was justified in the seminary but not in liberal arts programs. On the other hand, I had to admit, theories, methods, approaches, when applied to people without clothes in "exotic" societies, seemed to leave my students cold; but, applied to the Bible, these theories, methods, and approaches seemed suddenly and continually relevant. That is to say, there was no discernible interest in whether Durkheim was right about the Australian aborigines because no student had any immediate stake in the outcome, but apply Durkheim to the most arcane passages in Leviticus—and the interest became both palpable and universal. So, despite all reservations, I have found myself, each year, offering courses on the Bible or introducing biblical materials into every course taught. But, this strategic move presented its own problem. Beyond the vague defense that the Bible is (or, is thought to be) a "classic" text, and beyond the clear sense that it was a text my students felt strongly about (even if never read), I had no satisfactory rationale for this focus, no way to put to rest my earlier suspicions.

All of this changed twenty years ago, with the publication in the *Journal of the American Academy of Religion [JAAR]* of W. C. Smith's article, "The Study of Religion and the Study of the Bible."[3] For myself, as a teacher, this short piece has had the most decisive effect. It proposes nothing less than a Copernican Revolution with respect to the academic situation of the Bible. Consequently, I have tried, these past twenty years, in a yearlong sequence, "The Bible in Western Civilization," to respond to Smith's challenge in terms of the Jewish and Christian Bibles over the *longue durée* with comparative materials from the ancient Near Eastern, Late Antique, Islamic, and Mormon traditions.

Recall Smith's main argument. After beginning with some observations on the implications of the "transition from the seminary to the liberal arts department as a locus of inquiry," Smith turns to the "field of Bible as illustration," challenging first what he sees as the prevailing, unsophisticated "hermeneutic of suspicion." The second challenge is the center of gravity of the essay: a critique of the antiquarianism of much biblical study which focuses on the prehistory of the Bible, but never its subsequent history.

"The first point, then, is to see the Bible not merely as a set of ancient documents or even as a first- and second-century product but as a third-century, and twelfth-century, and nineteenth-century and contemporary agent" (134). That is to say, as a history which goes forward rather than backward, in his oft-repeated phrase, "the history of the Bible over the past twenty centuries," with a recommended comparativist introduction on "scripture as a generic phenomenon."

This second challenge is framed within a set of reflections on the historical-critical study of the Bible. Smith makes the accurate observation that this study should not serve as the taken-for-granted starting point of biblical studies but should be seen as "part of the nineteenth and early twentieth century history of Christian handling of Scripture." That is to say, "J" or "Q" are not tenth-century B.C. or first-century A.D. Palestinian artifacts, they are artifacts of nineteenth- and twentieth-century European thought. They stand towards the end rather than the beginning of the "history of the Bible over the past twenty centuries." [As an analogue, I recall asking Mircea Eliade why his beloved "primitives" (codeword, "archaic") had made no appearance in the first three volumes of his projected four-volume *Histoire des croyances et des idées religieuses.* "Because, Jonathan, they did not enter the history of the major religions until the sixteenth century." That is to say, the "archaic" is a discovery of the modern era. In light of this, I have often toyed with the idea of constructing a course about the West and its "others" built around the chronology of when we became interested in them. It is a significantly different time line than the one we are accustomed to—for example, the Sumerians would not appear until some seventy years ago.]

Because Smith can never leave well enough alone, because he has a mind that always rotates a thought one more (frequently unanticipated) turn, he does not stop here, but goes on to relate this historical/antiquarian interest to the conflict of myth and history, as well as the recession of the former.

Outside of the minor, technical quibble that Smith's suggestion of putting *in illo tempore* at the top or margin of King James' versions of the Bible would not constitute a replacement of the historical/chronological by the mythic (the phrase, after all, in the Vulgate of Luke 2:1 is, despite Eliade, in the service of an attempt at precise dating), I do not think Smith goes far enough. For, in the hands of the sixteenth-century Christian reformers (as with the nineteenth-century Jewish reformers), historical criticism was introduced precisely to serve a mythic project, the reactualization of the original "purity" of the "primitive, apostolic church." (One of the rare, positive uses of the term "primitive" in Western religious discourse.) That is to say, the earliest reformers used the New Testament as a standard to judge the degree to which Roman Catholicism had degenerated into "paganism." What they did not anticipate was that the following generations would take the very same techniques and apply them to the New Testament itself, thereby judging the degree to which some parts had degenerated from, or accreted to, the "original, pure faith." I know of no "native" myth more wedded to a cyclical view of history and to a recovery of pristine first times than that of the Reformation. But this is a matter I have dealt with elsewhere.

My major concern in this essay is to defend W. C. Smith from W. C. Smith and to suggest that his constant use, in the 1971 *JAAR* article, of the singular "The Bible" and "The Church" commits the same sort of reification, the same sort of misplaced concreteness, he has elsewhere warned against. In a sense, the Bible is still in the process of formation, as witnessed to by the number of candidates that would arise to the request: "Will the real Bible please stand up."

This is of no little concern to me, for, among the anachronisms I need to deal with when working with my students, is that the Bible is something which everyone can own and can read—a singular but infinitely replicable artifact that can be liberated from any hotel room in North America. (The only other book to attain this latter status, the classified phone directory, announces its difference and diversity on its cover and with every page). That is to say, I want to suggest that the Bible is not a nominal entity, and surely not a singular one, it is (in Smith's terminology) at best an adjectival or an adverbial construction. It was so in the beginning; it remains so today.

As Smith, in his *JAAR* article, repeatedly affirms his inclination to be "historical," I will focus briefly on that aspect of this issue.

As in the odd-sounding but common statement, Jesus was most likely born in six B.C. (!), the place to start is with the fact that "the Bible" is, at the very least, a post-biblical formulation. That is to say, no individual biblical text ever entertained the notion that it was fated, at some later date, to be placed together with others. Thus, while individual books may or may not contain warrants for themselves—ranging from letters from heaven, or claims to revelation, to ideas of accurate transmission or comparability—there is no internal warrant for the Bible as a whole. Nor does the arrangement of its components exhibit any coherent rationale (although some subsections arguably do), mixing together, as it does, principles of generic, statistical, and chronological order. The collection is post-biblical; the warrants are extra-biblical. This latter is best illustrated by the category of inspiration which plays no role in any biblical text and which comes to prominence only in apologetic arguments for biblical translations (first, the Septuagint, most strongly in Philo; then the Vulgate, most strongly in Augustine).

To borrow a strategy from Smith, even the terminology displays this. The singular terms *TANAKH* and *BIBLE* are late medieval terms. (*Biblia* is, itself, a plural, transformed, as with *opera*, in late vulgar Latin usage, into a singular.) The earlier Christian term, *bibliotheca*, emphasizes the motley, open-ended collection. The Hebrew *Torah* is scarcely exhausted by a particular collection of texts. The question of to what extent the *bibliotheca* could be seen as a (singular) *biblia* was enhanced twice, in Christian thought and imagination, by technology: first, the early and overwhelming Christian acceptance to the innovation of the codex which allowed disparate materials to be bound together with common covers and folio size. (This was far different for early Judaism. It could conceive of neither singularity nor closed canon so long as the material representation remained an armload of separate scrolls. Hence the rabbinic debates, often confused with canonicity, over what order the reading of the separate scrolls should follow.) The second innovation was printing which, by eliminating the diversity of hands, by facilitating indices, by enabling reproducibility, fostered the conviction of unity, indeed, of singular authorship. It should be noted that this reproducibility and identity was, post-print, no small problem for commercial Bible printers seeking a comparative advantage for their product which was, after all, identical to that of their competitors. The solution, as with soap powder, was found in varying the packaging and in the diversity of extra-biblical materials each edition included.

The plain fact is that, despite much ingenuity, there is no convincing theory for the origin of the notion of a collection or of a canon. To take up the Hebrew Bible first, there are no clear social loci in ancient Israel for all of the sorts of "books" that were eventually gathered together. Some of the historiographic materials may well have been situated in the royal court; most of the narrative and legal materials seem to be housed in (late) learned circles; the prophetic materials may well come from small groups of devotees, but no biblical materials can be located with respect to the most dominant religious and political institution, the Temple, although Temple traditions and laws were clearly preserved in extra-biblical materials. There is no social, political, religious, or functional niche for a collection like the Bible.

The best that can be said is that sources such as the Elephantine papyri show an almost total ignorance, in the 5th century B.C., of the texts and traditions that will later be called biblical, and that this is matched, in the same period, by the mutual ignorance of one sort of biblical material to another (e.g., the relative lack of references to the patriarchs, to Moses, or to the law at Sinai outside of their major narratives in the Pentateuch).

Beginning with the 3rd century B.C., connected with no particular historical event, although possibly related to wider disaporic formations, there are multiple witnesses to processes of collection, though not, I think to canon (the final fixing of a canon at Yavneh post-70 A.D. is an exploded pious fiction): (1) The Chronicler tradition as a replacement Bible from Adam to Ezra. (2) The multiple manuscript traditions at Qumran. (3) The beginning of explicit commentary traditions. (4) Processes of translation. (5) Other replacement Pentateuchs such as the Enoch Pentateuch, Jubilees, perhaps 11Q Temple Scroll, and the Samaritan Pentateuch.

(6) Expanded definition of the time span of prophecy which allowed *pesharim* and proof from prophecy. And so forth. Yet, shortly thereafter, one sees evidence of parallel processes of decentering what will later be called the Hebrew Bible (chiefly in early rabbinic tradition) to be relaxed, still later, only under external influence (e.g., the Karaites in relation to Islam; the nineteenth-century Jewish reformers in relation to Lutheran Christianity).

The Christian case is somewhat different in that it had as its model and employed for two centuries as its Bible some sort of translated collection of Israelitic writings. Here, aided by the technology of the codex and impelled by its character as a voluntary association, with typical concern for both charter and boundaries (hence, "heresies"), the ideal of a canon, a scriptural "rule" was established although never successfully achieved. After all, the Epistle to the Laodiceans still appeared in a number of seventeenth-century printed New Testaments.

Without reviewing the history of the Christian canon, the present course of the so-called "ecumenical" Revised Standard Version (or the New Revised Standard Version) provides an instructive parable. While it will always be too long a Bible for the Syrian church, and too short for the Ethiopic, its subsequent editions, adding to the Protestant Bible the Apocrypha for the Roman Catholics, and even more texts for the Greek Orthodox and Slavonic communities, while retaining the Protestant order, has resulted in a Bible which, in fact, conforms to no one's Bible. An attempt at unity has here resulted in an eccentric singularity. There is simply no omnipurpose, omnicompetent Bible for an omnipresent Christendom. Rather, there are a variety of Bibles and Christianities which exhibit varying degrees of "fit."

Other, more particular phenomena might be pointed to which suggest that, whatever Bible one chooses, some parts will always be "more equal than others." Technologically, this is revealed whenever an eglogadic lectionary (i.e., a noncontinual system of readings) is liturgically employed. In Judaism, this is the case with the prophets, reduced to the status of proto-rabbinic commentaries on particular passages of the Pentateuch (the latter read in a continuous system) in the *haftarah* books which only print out the relevant portion of the prophets in the order in which they are employed. While this was a considerable economy for hand-written manuscripts, the result is a text which is syntagmatically unreadable. The same phenomenon occurred, on a more massive scale, in the majority of Christianities which employ an entirely eglogadic lectionary: Thus, before print, handwritten *capitularies*, containing only the lections in their liturgical order, outnumber whole manuscript Bibles by some twenty to one, resulting, again, in a text which is unreadable serially, and which represents an unacknowledged fifth gospel, in this case one heard by more individuals than have ever read the full New Testament text.

Theologically, the same issue is represented by what will come to be called the "canon within the canon." Judaism's devalued prophetic books are reorganized as the culmination of the Christian Old Testament. The most central biblical text for Jews—Leviticus—has a long history of being the only biblical book not commented on in Christian commentary series. (A tradition of silence, in English, at least as old as the redoubtable International Critical Commentary.) To judge from Sunday morning radio, there are some Christian groups who seem to know of no other New Testament text than the Book of Revelation; there are other Christian groups who appear never to have heard of it. Or, one might point to the opposite phenomenon: the more literalist a community's reading of the Bible claims to be, the more allegorical it necessarily becomes, and its Bibles take more and more marginalia into the Bible itself. (Witness the various "study Bibles," giving Scofield and Ryrie pride of place.)

I could continue in this vein, reciting more of the history of diversity which serves as an illustration of the old conundrum that *Torah* most faithfully observes the first commandment, "Be fruitful and multiply." But I wish to reach for a different sort of conclusion.

What Smith's *JAAR* article opened for me, as I have struggled to design the sort of course he pointed to, has been a larger world of texts that I probably never would have otherwise read, texts which raise issues I never would have thought about. Texts and topics such as: (1) The lectionary systems and their complex chains of associations which produce a stunning variety of resonances. (2) The history of concordances and harmonies. (3) The relation of text to iconography. (4) The role of the lay reader (for which, in class, Columbus and La Peyrère have been the prime examples). And so forth. But I owe Smith a greater debt for having led me to that set of issues raised by the sort of diversities I have briefly rehearsed.

Thinking about these issues has, thus far, resulted, for me, in agenda rather than answers. They signal that, in some important sense, the Bible is still in the process of being constructed. This raises the issue (and parallel) of language as individuals and individual communities seek to find their distinctive voices (*parole*) through employing public coin of the realm (*langue*). And this suggests that reception history is, at the very least, as significant a study as genetic history. As with individual biblical manuscripts whose individuality ought not be reduced to a disassociated set of so-called "variants," measured against a hypothetic archetype, so too the largely reformist language of "post-" this or that, of accretion, is wide of the mark and falsifies the dynamics of tradition.

The diversities between religions have never struck me as particularly interesting. They are sheerly different; nothing more needs to be said. But the diversities within religious traditions who understand themselves in some sense to be the "same," or between traditions who understand themselves in some sense to be related, are differences which, at the very least, are potentially consequential. For, while these sorts of differences often lead to violence or to mutual anathematizing, they are the sorts of differences which most often lead to thought.

Notes

Method and Theory in the Study of Religion 4, no. 1–2 (1992): 98–105. Reprinted by permission.

1. Wilfred Cantwell Smith, *The Meaning and End of Religion: A New Approach to the Religious Traditions of Mankind* (New York: Macmillan, 1963).
2. On the pedagogical centrality of definitions, see "Approaching the College Classroom," 6; "The Introductory Course: Less Is Better," 17; and "Re-Forming the Undergraduate Curriculum," 94–95.—Ed.
3. *Journal of the American Academy of Religion* 39, no.2 (June 1971): 131–140. I have reflected further on the importance of Smith's article in J. Z. Smith, "Teaching the Bible in the Context of General Education," *Teaching Theory and Religion* 1 (1998): 73–78 and idem., "Religion and Bible," *Journal of Biblical Literature* 128 (2009): 5–27.

4

Here and Now: Prospects for Graduate Education

THERE SEEMS TO BE a curious embarrassment with respect to the topic of graduate education. While many faculty are well-scarred veterans of long and elaborate discussions of general or departmental undergraduate curricula, most are rank amateurs when it comes to discussions of graduate education. To be sure, we sometimes fiddle with details, change the examination structure, work out possibilities for substitutions of languages. We are accustomed to worrying about employment for our students going out, and the number and quality of our students coming in. But it is rare that we discuss the enterprise as a whole, or call it into question.

At first glance this appears plausible, especially insofar as we continue to identify graduate education with the dissertation. In most academic convocations, there is a revealing difference in ceremonial formulae. The candidates for doctoral degrees are commended for having successfully completed an original piece of research which contributes to knowledge in a particular field; the candidates for bachelors' degrees are commended for having successfully completed a program of studies prescribed by the faculty. Doctoral studies appear to result in a clear product—a monograph. Undergraduate studies are a process, a program. The former has a concrete and visible terminus; the latter, an artificial interruption. As long as we do not subject the doctoral formula to a set of rude questions, there is something self-evident about the tangible result of graduate studies. So long as we focus on the dissertation, the kinds of educational issues often raised with respect to undergraduate programs seem carping, idiosyncratic, and irrelevant. A piece of work is a piece of work, nothing more needs to be said. The dissertation is self-justifying, complete in itself. In Johan Huizinga's formulation: "It is quite unnecessary for each monograph to justify itself.... An entity in the cosmos, it has within itself the same right to exist as every blackbird that sings and every cow that eats grass."[1]

From such a vantage point, the curriculum leading to the doctoral degree can be reduced to a "need-to-know" basis. The model of doctoral studies appears to be that of the tutorial or apprenticeship. The more general requirements seem to exist only as prolegomena to the act of focus, to the definition of the terminal task, or to serve as ancillaries to it.

While I suspect that I might get broad agreement on such a notion of graduate studies *sub specie dissertationis*, the burden of my argument in this essay will be against such a view, both with respect to the academy in general, and with respect to the study of religion in particular (the latter being the context I best understand for graduate studies in Judaism).

With respect to the academy, it would be my contention that the focus on the dissertation is, in far too many programs, irresponsible and unrealistic. Despite striking corporate and individual exceptions, the academy does not appear to be an enterprise of sustained scholarship. The bulk of productive, important, and ever-maturing research is done by a small minority. If we count only such research as achieves publication, the minority contracts even further. For example, it has been estimated that some 10 percent of the faculty members in the United States are responsible for more than 85 percent of the scholarly publications. I take one implication of this to be that, in more instances than we may care to admit, a student is directed in his or her dissertation by a faculty member whose only significant act of research was his or her dissertation.

A significant number of faculty members are not competent to direct the kind of sustained research that results in the monographic dissertation; a good many graduate students are not yet ready and certainly most are not well trained for the kind of sustained research that results in the monographic dissertation. As a result, the faculty member and the graduate student appear to enter into a covenant of banality with the following sorts of results.

In far too many dissertations from a variety of institutions that it has been my lot to read, the initial chapter is often devoted to a review of previous scholarship that witnesses to little more than a capacity to use, indifferently, a modest number of bibliographical tools. Rarely is there critical evaluation. The principle appears to be: if it was said, it is worth noting. Rarely is there the capacity to account for the various results of one's predecessors, whether in terms of some wider history of ideas or of disciplines, or some sociology of knowledge. Figures are allowed to cohabit the page who would assassinate each other if placed together in a room, so varied are their presuppositions, methods, and interests. This the author of the dissertation has failed to detect, having only read the "relevant" paragraph or page—if, indeed, the reference was not cribbed. In such a chapter, a motley list of sorts may have been achieved, but not history, not the winning of a useful historical-critical perspective.

Turning next to the body of this putative dissertation, one rapidly discovers why the more leisurely and discursive term "dissertation" has come to replace the more combative and assertive term "thesis." For there is rarely an argument, at least rarely an argument conducted by any logical or dialectical rules. No clarity on the roles of definitions, classifications, and explanations—the central building blocks of academic discourse. No sense of what constitutes an objection, of "what counts." No precision in stipulating a domain. No painful and argued decisions of choice. All is equal. Everything is of equivalent gravity. All that is required is for it to have been "there."[2]

Alongside of this inability to argue and to accept responsibility for decisions of inclusion and exclusion, there is often a bland nodding to authority. The rule seems to be: do not say something yourself if a quotation, no matter how dubious the source, can be found. And, thanks to modern xerography, make the quotation as long as possible, and leave the reader free to choose for himself what portion he finds relevant or interesting. (If all else fails, the rule appears to continue, state in a footnote, "it is interesting to note..." but never specify in what the interest lies.)

The "concluding" chapter is precisely not that. It does not venture any conclusions, at least in a form that might advance research. Rather it reviews and summarizes the previous chapters, and frequently promises subsequent work which will be (alas) more of the same. There are no proposals as to the implications of the research for the definition of the scholarly field. No predictions as to the necessary entailments for others' work. No specifications as to the degree to which the results achieved, the questions asked, the methods employed, the data chosen are to be taken as exemplary of a wider range of topics, or what modifications might have to be made if they were to be elsewhere applied. This, I suspect, is due to the fact that the series of intellectual tasks and objectives just proposed imply a trained self-consciousness that is, more often than not, utterly lacking. There has been no explicit training in such matters. All has been left to the accidents of osmosis and mimesis. Instead, there is an overwhelming

sense of relief to the final chapter—on the part of student, professor, and
reader—at having achieved the end of a period of time and a task which
will be looked back upon with frustration and distaste.

In presenting such a composite dissertation, I have, of course, exag-
gerated. But not by so great a degree as to allow the illusion of comfort.
The picture is bleak, but its bleakness, given the present state of the academy, was predictable. In the undeniable truism of the cybernetic sage:
"Garbage in, garbage out."

The reader will have noted that, in so caricaturing this imaginary but
all-too-typical dissertation, I have provided, as well, an implicit formulation of a generic description of what ought to be the content of graduate
studies.[3] That is to say, whatever else they learn, graduate students should
be exposed to their disciplinary past in such a way as to learn the art of
critical evaluation and to gain the ability to account for this past in terms
of a broadly based historical consciousness. They must learn the context
of their second-order tradition as well as they have mastered the primary
texts, and the difficult art of evaluating each in terms of the other as well as
in terms of historical perspectives and intellectual principles. They should
learn, through explicit attention to rules and by the careful study of examples, the crafts of argument and dialectics, the art of making things count
and of determining what counts, as well as more philosophical issues relative to the types and status of definitions, taxonomies, and explanations.
They should be capable of stipulating why their chosen data are exemplary
in terms of clearly stated, well-formulated issues central to their academic
discipline. And they should be taught ways of "cost accounting" for the
decisions of choice and interpretation that they make.

Such concerns, and there are others which might have equal claim for
attention, are not the domain of any particular discipline or field of study.
They are what constitutes an endeavor as academic. They constitute the elements of a general education at the graduate level. If the dissertation is to
continue to be perceived as the culminating point of graduate studies, the
students must learn, along with the appropriate field-specific skills, the
generic arts of arguing a thesis and specifying its implications. And they
must learn these arts through courses explicitly devoted to this end. We
cannot continue our present fixation on the dissertation without a proper
curriculum which balances both the generic claims of the academy and
the more specific claims of a given field of inquiry.[4]

The focus on the dissertation, and the concomitant reduction of the
curriculum to a "need-to-know" basis, has had a further negative effect

on the academy. For all the weight placed on the enterprise of sustained (and, frequently, solitary) scholarship in graduate programs, the majority of their faculty, and the majority of their students, teach and will teach heavily in undergraduate programs. This is all but unacknowledged in the formalities of graduate education.

The fact remains that, despite much talk about the relationship of teaching to research, the recognition that the majority of the positions in the future will be in undergraduate programs, and the widespread employment of graduate students in instructional roles, there is little explicit attention to teaching in most graduate programs. What occurs, with heroic exceptions, seems to take place largely by accident or as a result of an uncommon, and ultimately countereducational, faith in imitation and trial and error. I would think that it would be possible to design teaching requirements as a part of the Ph.D.—at the very least, to require the submission of a proposed syllabus for a course of the student's design with a written rationale for the various elements and pedagogic strategies, or the preparation of a series of critical reviews of the major undergraduate textbooks in one's field of interest, with the development of seminars or colloquia in support of these. Such requirements, alongside the more usual modes of in-service training, especially if the latter included analyzing the pedagogics and performance of a course as well as its subject matter, would be a modest beginning. I would hope for a time when it would be as routine a matter to deny a degree to a student who failed a teaching requirement as it would to one who failed some linguistic or special-area examination.

Thus far, I have focused on the teleology of graduate studies: the dissertation and the teaching. But this is not what is, for me, at stake. Through such a focus I hoped to suggest that what we most lack in so many instances is a *conception of a graduate program,* a graduate curriculum. To put this another way, we appear to do best, and to have expended most effort, at the beginning and end of graduate instruction, at the crafting of the introductory course and at the intense mentor relationship. What we lack is a graceful *middle range.*[5] In program after program, in field after field, I find no rationale for what is offered between a student's first course and the moment when he or she has fulfilled all course requirements. The variety of courses may be interesting, they may be well taught, they may be responsibly undertaken. But they do not cohere, they are rarely cumulative, they often seem ignorant of one another. They reflect well the varied, individual interests of the faculty, but they do not set forth some corporate understanding of a discipline or field, they reflect no institutional judgment. They appear to initiate into idiosyncratic styles, not into a sense of a profession or craft. What structures there are most closely resemble undergraduate distribution requirements and may be subjected to the same criticism: the students are being asked, unaided, to integrate what the faculty will not.[6]

If we are to continue as an academy, we cannot remain so careless of the large range of courses which stretch in-between the introduction and the dissertation. It is here that our students spend the majority of their time; it is here that the intellectual and professional context of one's future work is formed; it is here that a discipline is forged; and, for these reasons, it is here that the curricular discussions and corporate decisions of the future will have to be focused.

Against this general background, the particular matter of religious studies at the graduate level may be seen more clearly. Indeed, the matters raised above become more pressing because of the peculiar history of religious studies within the academy.[7]

For most of Western educational history, religious studies were carried on within theological faculties, within seminaries, where the appropriate emphasis was on the study and transmission of the received tradition by adherents of that tradition, where the appropriate goal was the training of a learned clergy. This was changed, in theory, on October 1, 1877, when the Dutch Universities Act separated the theological faculties at the four state universities from the Dutch Reformed Church. For the first time in Western academic history, there were established two parallel possibilities for the study of religion: a humanistic mode within the secular academy which might have as its object of thought some *generic conception of religion*; and a theological course of study within the seminary largely devoted to one of the religions. The original draft of the legislation had proposed to call the new department the Faculty of Religious Sciences, but, after much debate and compromise, the older title, Faculty of Theology, was retained. Nevertheless, dogmatics and practical theology, the central core of a Protestant theological education, were removed from the curriculum, henceforth to be taught only in the seminaries. Their place was taken by a new program in history of religions which was assumed to be more "neutral and scientific."

France followed soon after. In 1884, the French ministry of education abolished the state Catholic theological faculties and, a year later, replaced them (with a sense of Gallic irony, in the very same building) by the "fifth section of religious sciences" as part of the École Pratique des Hautes Études. Religious studies were thus placed alongside the other four sections: mathematics, the physical sciences, the biological sciences, and the historical-philological sciences. The minister of public education charged the new faculty: "We do not wish to see the cultivation of polemics, but of critical research. We wish to see the examination of texts, not the discussion of dogmas."[8]

In 1904, the University of Manchester, which was unusual among British universities in being nondenominational, in applying no confessional tests to either students or faculty, established a new theological faculty which taught both theological subjects and comparative religions, but which excluded courses in systematic theology and the history of Christian doctrine.

Few other European countries followed this pattern. In most of Europe, religious studies were a part of the divine sciences; the degree was a theological degree.

In the United States, until some twenty years ago, a sequential pattern prevailed. That is to say, a doctoral degree in religious studies (whether from a seminary or a university) had, more often than not, the prerequisite of a bachelor of divinity degree from a seminary.

With few exceptions, it was not until the rise of graduate programs in state universities, a development which largely followed the 1963 United States Supreme Court *School District of Abington v. Schempp* decision (374 U.S. 203), that the parallel course of study, instituted a century earlier in Holland, became a widespread possibility in this country.

I have rehearsed this well-known history in order to make two points. First, *the debates over the nature of the academic study of religion have rarely been substantive; they have been largely political and tactical.* That is to say, they have been informed by concerns not so much indigenous to the academy as appropriate to legislative bodies and legal questions of the relationship between church and state. Second, until recently, *the graduate study of religion was preceded, in the typical student's career, by a course of postbaccalaureate professional study within a theological faculty.*

Let me address this second point first, because it is crucial for the understanding of the present dilemma of religious studies within the academy, dominated as it is by Protestant concerns and models. It is this second point as well which exacerbates, for religious studies, the more generic problems sketched above with respect to graduate education.[9]

The issue was put with precision by Claude Welch in his 1971 comprehensive report *Graduate Education in Religion: A Critical Appraisal* (a report which, by the way, despite the harsh criticism with which it was greeted in some quarters, wears exceedingly well).

> What is to take the place of the theological degree [i.e., the B.D.] as the base on which advanced studies in religion are built? A distinctive feature of the tradition of graduate education in religion is that there were important common bases. The traditional route to the doctoral degree for Protestant, Catholic and Jew alike, was through the seminary curriculum. This is still true of the majority of students in Ph.D. studies...[but] increasing numbers of students are going directly into graduate work in religion with indifference or even disdain for study in the professional theological schools. The new trend poses a problem, however, because whatever the merits or demerits of the professional orientation of the seminary curriculum, the traditional route did provide both depth and breadth within the limits of a major religious tradition on which it was possible to build real specialization. There was, in other words, a common base or core of study.... But, if the movement to by-pass the theological degree continues to grow—and it will—and if "religious studies" is to be defined as other than strictly Catholic studies or Jewish studies or Buddhist studies or Hindu studies, the situation is genuinely critical. Either we fall into a chaos of simply unrelated investigations, in which no one can finally talk to anyone else, or we search for new patterns of coherence.[10]

The academic study of religion is not taught in most public high schools. The graduate study of religion cannot rely on coherent undergraduate religion programs to replace the lost though limited coherence of the theological degree. If one surveys the various undergraduate curricula and course syllabi, in most cases there is little that is common beyond some components adapted from the seminaries. If one surveys the textbooks, there is overwhelming evidence for religious studies' lack of a "second-order" tradition.[11] Each textbook that strives for generality represents either an idiosyncratic attempt at incoherent synthesis (e.g., the texts authored by Fred Streng) or an encyclopedia of trivia (e.g., the shockingly widely used text by John Noss). There is no guarantee that any topic or figure treated in one textbook will be even mentioned in another which claims to introduce the same field. All is ad hoc. All appears to be improvisation.

What we have not faced as a profession is that our "second-order" tradition at the graduate level was, for more than a century, provided by the B.D. or its equivalent. Having had the luxury of this common core upon which to build a graduate curriculum, we irresponsibly failed to provide its equivalent once this prerequisite was jettisoned. Having had the additional luxury of this negative contrast against which to position the academic study of religion, we have now lost our "common enemy." (These problems are made more difficult by the introduction of non-Western religions into the curriculum, taught by individuals largely trained in philological or area studies programs which appear to lack any principles of coherence beyond the ability to decipher a non-Roman alphabet.)

The bachelor's degree cannot provide this coherence. The undergraduate programs will not be brought into order except by the models provided and the teachers trained by the graduate faculties. But these have been unwilling to work at the challenge of providing a new core.

There is an additional reason for this failure of nerve within religious studies. To develop this I must reiterate a previous point. Religious studies have almost never defined themselves in a substantive manner; rather, they have been preoccupied with politics and tactics.

The issues raised by the large literature on the academic study of religion since the late 1950s, when religious studies programs within state universities first became possible, have been largely those of *legitimacy*. The putative separation of church and state, as well as the concomitant suspicion that religion could not be addressed academically, made these matters urgent. Hence the endless discussion of questions of objectivity and subjectivity, of the descriptive and the normative, and other such matters that would be incomprehensible apart from a political situation in which legitimacy is conferred not by the academy as a result of public scholarly achievement and utility, but rather by legalistic formulations that license the teaching "about" religion but not the teaching "of" religion (to crudely paraphrase Mr. Justice Goldberg's historic, but equally crude, opinion).

Even our more overtly substantive discussions are suspect as being, in fact, political and tactical. One does not have to be a Marxist to discern some economic substrate beneath our ideological formulations. For example, in the expansionist 1960s, we argued that religion was an irreducible, sui generis phenomenon. Translation: a separate department of religion was required. In the contractive late 1970s and early 1980s, we have argued that religious studies are uniquely "polymethodical" (or, as one colleague facetiously suggests, drawing on the old folk tune, we "sing polymethodoodle all the day"). Translation: an ill-willed provost cannot dispense with religious studies, because he can't find them. They are intercalated with the humanities and social sciences.[12]

Of more gravity, if we were to develop a consensus on the academic study of religion such that a proper curriculum could be generated, we would have to recognize that behind all the questions of alleged substance (as well as those of law and politics) lies a set of unexamined, certainly Christian, chiefly Protestant, presuppositions which have guaranteed that the majority of the religious phenomena of mankind will remain forever un-understandable. In so many respects, seen from the perspective of a general study of religion, Protestantism is an exception which requires explanation; it cannot be used as a model for explanation.

The preoccupation with the categories of belief and faith, the primacy of individual experience, the distinction between a sphere of religion and a sphere of civility, the derogation of ritual, the primacy of the text—these, and almost every other category developed internally within the field of religious studies, are dependent upon and incomprehensible without peculiarly Protestant presuppositions. Nor, when we go "outside," is there much difference. That we appropriate sociologies with categories such as charisma and routinization, church and sect; that we find models in the allegedly anthropological (but, in fact, covertly theological) tradition of Parsons, Geertz, and Bellah, are only to meet these same Protestant presuppositions but slightly translated into another language. Furthermore, by being "religious" rather than theological, these old theological agenda are cut off from all responsibility to a community consensus and to a received tradition. Within the "secular" academy, they are free to be irresponsible. An individual theology is a contradiction in terms, yet it is precisely this which, in the academy, often passes for and provides the agendum of some theory of religion.

I have no particular interest in the study of Judaism, except insofar as it can contribute to the enterprise of developing the general study of religion. The categories that may be developed with respect to the Jewish materials may be distant enough to call into question the traditional categories of religious studies, yet related enough for discourse rather than mere juxtaposition to be possible. I am not interested in a Jewish theory of religion (whatever that would be), or in categories so crafted as to apply only to Jewish phenomena (however they be defined). But I am concerned with the possibility of developing a critique of our present presuppositions.

And here the study of Judaism in the academy might be of some modest aid. As I have written in another context:

> The interest of the student of religion in Judaism cannot depend on apologetic, historical or demographic reasons. That is to say, the interest in Judaism for the imagination of religion cannot be merely because it is "there," because it has played some role in our collective invention of Western civilization, or because some students of religion happen to be Jews. Rather it is because of the peculiar position of Judaism within the larger framework of the imagining of Western religion: close, yet distant; similar, yet strange; "occidental," yet "oriental"; common place, yet exotic. This tension between the familiar and the unfamiliar, at the very heart of the imagining of Judaism, has enormous cognitive power. It invites, it requires, comparison. Judaism is foreign enough to most students of religion for comparison and interpretation to be necessary; it is close enough for comparison and interpretation to be possible. By virtue of its tensive situation between the near and the far, Judaism provides an important test case for central methodological issues such as definition and comparison besides illuminating the larger areas of imagination, self-consciousness and choice crucial to the academic study of religion.[13]

It is only when such central issues and larger questions are corporately and explicitly addressed that we may begin to develop a core and a curriculum for graduate studies and gain explanatory power for the more particular investigations represented by the dissertation. If not now, when? If not here, where?

Notes

Jacob Neusner, ed., *New Humanities and Academic Disciplines: The Case of Jewish Studies* (Madison: University of Wisconsin Press, 1984), 33–45. © 1984 by the Board of Regents of the University of Wisconsin System. Reprinted courtesy of the University of Wisconsin Press.

1. Johan Huizinga, "The Task of Cultural History," in *Men and Ideas: Essays by Johan Huizinga*, trans. James S. Holmes and Hans van Marie (New York: Meridian, 1959), 22.
2. Compare with the extended account of college work as "training in argument about interpretations," in "Puzzlement," esp. 123–34.—Ed.

3. Compare this curricular description with that in "Basic Problems in the Study of Religion," 21–24.—Ed.

4. As long as present practice holds in the hiring of faculty, I have little hope for the alteration of the notion that graduate study is a preparation for the dissertation. But I applaud proposals such as the one from a department at a major research university to keep the traditional monographic dissertation in place for those who elect it, but to offer an alternative for those who do not. Analyzing the kinds of tasks performed by the scholar-teacher in the contemporary academy, this proposal suggested three requirements which might be fulfilled in lieu of the dissertation: (1) the preparation of a scholarly article on a focused topic that would be accepted by a refereed journal; (2) the preparation of a long, generalizing chapter on a genre or historical period of the sort that might appear in a standard multivolumed reference work (such as the *Cambridge History*); and (3) the presentation of a lecture open to the general public as well as to the academy on some topic of interest and concern growing out of the student's work. I am interested in recommending not so much the details as the impulse which lay behind this proposal—the recognition of a variety of roles in today's academic profession, not all of which are well served or tested for by the traditional monographic dissertation.

5. On the need for a "middle range," see also "Why the College Major?" 114.—Ed.

6. Smith's "iron law": see "Re-Forming the Undergraduate Curriculum," 94.—Ed.

7. For more extended accounts of this disciplinary history, see in this volume "Religious Studies: Whither (Wither) and Why?" 64–72 passim; also Jonathan Z. Smith, "A Twice-told Tale: The History of the History of Religions' History," in *Relating Religion: Essays in the Study of Religion* (Chicago: University of Chicago Press, 2004), 362–374.—Ed.

8. Eric J. Sharpe, *Comparative Religion: A History* (London: Duckworth, 1975), 122.

9. Compare the following discussion with "Religious Studies: Whither (Wither) and Why?" 64–65.—Ed.

10. Claude Welch, *Graduate Education in Religion: A Critical Appraisal* (Missoula: University of Montana Press, 1971), 21–22.

11. I owe the formulation of religious studies' lack of a "second-order tradition" to an unpublished paper by Walter Capps of the University of California, Santa Barbara.

12. Compare this discussion with "Religious Studies: Whither (Wither) and Why?" 68–69.—Ed.

13. Jonathan Z. Smith, *Imagining Religion* (Chicago: University of Chicago Press, 1982), xii.

5

Connections

HOW COULD ONE refuse an invitation to meditate aloud on the question of connections at the outset of our meeting when the issue was so fetchingly framed by Jim Wiggins? He called, several months ago, to tell me that the Program Committee of the American Academy of Religion (AAR) had just met, here in Anaheim, and concluded that there appeared to be nothing programmatic about our annual meeting. Jim recalled that I had once suggested that if our present course of atomization continued, allowing, at any given moment, no less than sixteen simultaneous fifteen-minute sound bites (with an equivalent number in the parallel Society of Biblical Literature [SBL] meeting), the AAR might do better (and save some money) simply to provide each member with the tools that enable solitary vice, with an individual phone booth and a credit card, and give up the fiction of a plenum. "Is there," Jim asked, "anything unifying, any contrary centripetal impulse governing our activities as an academy?" In asking me to address this question in what he, then, termed a "kick-off speech" (now pleonastically dignified as an "inaugural opening address"), Jim left me with the rueful sense that I was to attempt a task similar to that undertaken by the artist Christo (itself a not insignificant name), wrapping gauze around an already existent and somewhat recalcitrant object. The blurb in the *Religious Studies News* did nothing to dispel this unease. The auguries do not bode well. After all, in its recent mail survey of members' "primary research," the AAR found it necessary to set out nine "geographic areas," eighteen "traditions," eleven "approaches," and twenty-eight "subject areas," with the doubtless unintended ironic result that if you, like me, understood *religion* to be the object of your studies, you had to write it in, under the rubric "other"!

I chose the title, "Connections," in part because it shares with "religion" the root sense of "binding" (although built on a different root, **ned* rather than *leigh*), but more particularly in homage to that remarkable BBC and PBS series on the history of science and technology, James Burke's *Connections*. Eschewing the usual picture of a process of lineal inevitable development, or the heroism of individual geniuses and inventors, Burke portrays a more haphazard process, resembling *bricolage*, that becomes clear and necessary only in retrospect.[1] Our coherence, arguably, is of a similar character.

Let me begin with two historical snapshots. Despite the short shrift given to the rationale for the change of name from the already renamed National Association of Biblical Instructors (NABI) to the American Academy of Religion in our founding document of 1964,[2] the latter title has proved prescient. With the benefit of hindsight, it is possible to maintain that the three elements in our title, taken together, constitute a first mapping of our commonality. We are an indigenously American enterprise, a field of study that has chosen, and is comfortable with, the so-called "secular" academy as a setting and our neighbors in the human sciences as colleagues and conversation partners for our work, a work directed towards a theoretical object: religion. This could not have been said fifty years ago. The distance we have collectively traveled can be marked by contrasting a complaint from the beginning of our "turn," indeed, from the very first paragraph of the first issue of the *Journal of Bible and Religion* (the ancestor of the *Journal of the American Academy of Religion* [*JAAR*]) with the celebration of the same "turn" in a remark at our seventy-fifth anniversary banquet in Chicago fifty-one years later. In 1933, Chester Warren Quimby, in his presidential address, lamented:

> That all is not well with the teaching of the English Bible is a well-known and all too bitter axiom. The early hope that we [NABI] might become an influential national society has failed. The Southern section—the very core of the "Bible Belt"—was stillborn. The Central and Western sections have become vague societies of religion. The Bible departments of our own section are fast changing to Departments of religion, so that now although we only are left they are seeking our life to take it away.[3]

By way of contrast, in 1984, Charles Long proclaimed, with barely concealed delight, that, as a learned society, we have moved "from the clarity of the Book to the chaos of discourse about religion."[4] Although the first quotation denigrates, and the second celebrates, our "turn," their language is wholly congruent. The result of the "turn" is "vague societies of religion" and the "chaos of discourse about religion." Our scholarly "turn" is understood by both to be from a sharp focus on an object, the Bible, understood, authoritatively, to be religious, to a highly contested construct: religion.

The study of religion, especially at its more advanced levels, is unique among the human sciences in its bi-locality, often denoted in our professional shorthand by the dualism seminary/university. While this bi-locality is not innocent of implications for the question of unity (to which I shall want to return), here it helps clarify the reasons for the differing evaluations by Quimby and Long. For the focus on objects and authority is appropriate to the seminary; the insistence on construct and conflict is equally characteristic of the university.

I have been repeatedly struck by the force of this wider duality over the past year, as the Editorial Board, on behalf of the AAR, has struggled with the construction of the *HarperCollins Dictionary of Religion*, conceived as an analogue to the SBL's *Harper's Bible Dictionary* (*HBD*).[5] For beyond its physical dimensions and some technical matters of format, the analogy breaks down. Any Bible dictionary, by its very nature, working with an expansive yet delimited corpus, has as its conceptual spine a concordance, a list of every name, place, and thing mentioned in the Bible (in the case of *HBD*, every name used three or more times), to which is added a variety of historical and archeological terms conceived to have relevance to the age and setting of the books, as well as a traditional list of theological topoi. Whether merited or not, a positivistic rhetoric governs the enterprise, even when it is being most speculative. To quote the *HBD*'s preface:

> Because the articles represent great care in reaching conclusions only where the *evidence* will support such conclusions, much of what was once considered certain will be shown to rest on the smallest foundations of *factual* knowledge, while other things about which the reader may have been in confusion will be shown to have enough *evidence* to clear up the difficulties. Scholarship is an adventure in learning, in which *new facts* constantly open up new horizons of information, and the pages of this Dictionary reflect that adventure.[6]

Such a rhetoric would be sheerly impossible in our *Dictionary of Religion*. First of all, because there is no delimited corpus. It is our particular group of editors who create a canon—one that is responsive and

responsible to no other community than the academy—by their decisions on what to include and exclude. For example, in the assignments
for the *HarperCollins Dictionary of Religion*, the largest number of entries
(no surprise) refer to Christianity, but "new religions" will provide the
second-largest number. While one might argue (unsuccessfully, I believe)
that Christianity functions in a manner similar to a natural taxon, "new
religion" is clearly an artificial class, wholly the creation of the academy.
Secondly, because there is no empirical corpus, connections are not "at
hand." Terms do not "cluster" in documentary, geographical, or historical
space. There are no "given" metonymic or syntagmatic relations. Rather,
connections will have to be forged by the scholars' work. Terms can be
related only in intellectual space. Their relations will be metaphoric and
paradigmatic. Hence, there can be no concordance-like citation of textual loci to supply contextual meaning. Rather, each and every item will
have to be supplied with a cross-reference to an appropriate generic term
developed within the academic study of religion, which will serve as the
sole locus for their conjunction. Thirdly, this means that the *Dictionary
of Religion* will have to break with the archaic (though still puzzlingly
prevalent) notion that words name things. As the philosophical debate
over definitions has taught us, words refer to other words, and it is this
relationship that our *Dictionary* will have to explore and evaluate. Finally,
in a *Dictionary* that cannot, by its nature, celebrate "new horizons of information," the vistas it offers its readers must be the unfolding of questions
of interpretation. We must invite them, in Bill Green's precise formulation, to "use their intellects and imaginations to engage with previously
unconsidered peoples, texts, behaviors, experiences and ideas...[and] to
confront the previously unconsidered in their own assumptions and in
themselves" concerning religion.[7]

At stake is a view of the academic enterprise that challenges positivistic
notions of authority and facticity, a view that sees scholars as participating
endlessly in "negotiatory or transactional" processes. From this perspective,
a professional society, such as ours, is as much, if not more, a "forum" for
negotiating and renegotiating constructions of significance as it is a means
of transmitting "new information."[8] What we share are the intellectual
problems attendant on such an enterprise. In Richard Rorty's terminology,
we have chosen "solidarity," the participation in an ongoing "conversation"
and debate, over "Enlightenment" ideals of "objectivity" and agreement.[9]

I could continue in this vein and persist in using the proposed
Dictionary as an emblem for our endeavor. I could, for example, suggest,

as a thought experiment, constructing our annual meeting's program book in a manner analogous to the *Dictionary*. That is to say, alongside of maintaining the fiction, expressed by the majority of our organizational units, that our collective work is "naturally" divided by geographic areas,[10] chronological periods, or religious traditions, we might attempt a similar system of cross-references for each presentation, making it possible to read the program both serially and horizontally. To take up only one topos that it is my lot to be engaged with at this meeting, a session titled "Sacrifice, Religion, and Violence." A conservative count shows that some thirty-two papers in twenty-three sections directly address important aspects of this topic. Thirteen of them are clustered in four sections, three of which have the misfortune to be scheduled to meet at the same time later this afternoon. Such a retrospective cross-referencing is one way of tracing connections as well as fulfilling the intentions of the founders of the AAR, who, believing that "specialists in religion particularly require breadth,"[11] argued that the new academy "must establish generalizing as well as specializing resources."[12] Or, I could turn to the results of an informal analysis of the programs of the past ten annual meetings and of the contents of *JAAR* for the same period in an attempt to expose the set of tacit understandings which inform, but are rarely the objects of, our corporate discourse about religion. We seem, as a group, increasingly disinterested in talk of "religion in essence and manifestation," preferring, rather, to see religion as deeply embedded in human culture, history, and social formation. While notions of transcendence hover in the background, much of our speech appears to intend to claim that there is a religious "aspect," "approach," "perspective," or "dimension" to some subject or area of human experience and expression which has nonreligious dimensions as well. Eschewing past bold talk of the *sui generis*, the "religious" most frequently appears to be conceived as a sort of "extra-plus" (the "most integrative" is quite common), but we have no apparent interest in defining "religion." Indeed, if pressed, we seem to prefer the notion that it is indefinable. We have, increasingly, taken note of the "linguistic turn," but have used it more to support a highly generalized notion of *homo symbolicus* rather than any hard-edged structuralist or semiotic theory. While we are persistently concerned with the ethics of intercultural translation, we have no discernable concern with the theory of translation. All this is congruent with two deeply held positions: the one, a strong commitment to particularity, a sense of responsibility to the specificity and integrity of our diverse objects of study; the other, a strong reluctance to engage

with theory. Both of these positions have led to a surprising lack of interest, given our disciplinary history, in the comparative enterprise. Thus, in
our several sections, we frequently juxtapose materials but almost never
explicitly compare them. Our disinclination towards theory, however, has
not led us to embrace more empirical pursuits. Economics of religion,
survey research, and the like, have been cheerfully abandoned to the
Society for the Scientific Study of Religion. While statistically we are still
focused on the West, it is often without an articulated claim of privilege;
rather, a common-sense posture of respect for pluralism prevails. Of late,
the question of the relationship or priority of the insider and outsider has
been much discussed—but, this has neither sundered the field nor led to
major revisionary projects as it has, for example, in anthropology. Favored
figures come and go. Tillich remains the unacknowledged theoretician of
our entire enterprise. Durkheim has become interesting, but not Weber
and never Marx. Geertz still looms large, but not Lévi-Strauss, and no
longer Turner or Mary Douglas. In general, literary criticism has emerged
as the most interesting conversation partner, replacing symbolic anthropology and strands of continental philosophy.... I could go on and on,
and hope to gain your assent to the correspondence of my ethnography;
however, it is time to pause in order to revisit and re-vision Jim Wiggins's
original question in a way that will focus less on the matter of religion and
more on the nature of an academy.

Given what has already been said, it must be asked whether the question of unity and coherence is an appropriate one to ask of a professional
society that participates (regardless of the actual location of individual
members) fully in the ethos of the modern research university, conceived
as a sphere of contestation with an uncertain center and blurred boundaries, which has available to it, not processes of proof, but, rather, rhetorics
of persuasion, and to which the notion of some clarifying Pentecost can
appear only as a nostalgic fantasy? Is not the drive to unity more appropriate (to invoke our professional shorthand of bi-locality once again) to the
seminary and its agendum than to the university? Or, to put the question
another way, while our subject matter, religion, is often characterized by
imperialistic impulses towards totalism, determinism, integration, and
unification, need the study of religion mirror its subject matter in these
respects?

There are other, more general, reasons for raising the question of the
appropriateness of impulses towards unity. The nineteenth-century models of the research university (under which we still largely operate) owe

much to the sort of organizational thinking epitomized in Adam Smith's striking image of the pin factory: the notion of a number of specialists, each contributing her or his separate (and often idiosyncratic) labor to form a single knowledge product as it moves down the university's assembly line. This image was reinforced by a widely shared understanding of "the ways things are" which Alvin Toffler has wittily labeled "indust-reality," which extended the notion of the factory to the cosmos, the conviction that:

> The universe is an *assembled* reality, made of discrete parts put together in an assemblage. Matter can only be understood in terms of motion—i.e., movement through *space*. Events occur in a linear succession, a parade of events moving down the [assembly] line of time.[13]

While Marx might argue (correctly) that the result of the industrial model was "alienation," Durkheim, himself a major theoretician for the French educational system, asserted the faith of the turn-of-the-century academy that the inevitable interdependence of specialized labor resulted in "organic solidarity." Be this as it may, in our contemporary situation, decentralization and service functions, not the assembly line, are the regnant models of production. The nineteenth-century image of the university as a knowledge factory, as a "smokestack industry," would seem to doom it to be placed in the "rust belt" along with other, similar, anachronisms.

What appears to have emerged, in both industry and the academy as well as in the civic realm, are shifting congeries of special interest or single issue groups where, in contradistinction to the older linear and hierarchical model, everyone contributes to the particular task at hand and where the group will probably not outlast the task, thereby making its activities more closely akin to play than to work. In universities across the country, the traditional, vertical departmental organization is being permeated by crosscutting institutes, workshops, and the like. Individual scholars, typically, find their most intellectually profitable associations to be no longer within the fixed space of their campus, but rather in the highly mobile world of professional meetings and conferences, and they have transferred their loyalties accordingly, without, however, dismantling the departmental structure (which remains a convenience for receiving mail).[14] Extending the image of John Higham, the academy looks like

"a house in which the inhabitants are leaning out of the many open win-
dows gaily chatting with the neighbors, while the doors between the
rooms stay closed."[15]

Within the AAR, during the past decade, a parallel process has been
at work. The sometimes bewildering variety of "groups," "seminars," and
"consultations" often appear to generate more energy and attract more
interest than the traditional (and industrial) organization by "sections."
Indeed, the latter, with the introduction of "themes," has begun to imitate
the focused and ad hoc character of the former.[16]

If, in an effort to deparochialize ourselves (itself, one of the leading
impulses of the contemporary academy), we glance beyond our borders to
other professional meetings within the human sciences, we will swiftly
discern that their condition is analogous to ours. We will observe the presence of continued debate over a relatively few issues, all of which we share:
questions of objectivity/subjectivity, advocacy, and controversies concerning the interpretative privilege of the outside/insider. Indeed, two important histories of professional societies, one in history, the other in social
sciences, have been written around these themes.[17] This argument on
what is problematic leads one to suspect that these are intellectual issues
inherent in the academic enterprise itself and not indigenous to any particular field or subject matter.

On the other hand, observation of other professional societies and
meetings will show that fragmentation and centrifugal processes are
equally ubiquitous.

Item: The American Institute of Biological Sciences is, in fact, a hold-
ing company for more than forty distinct research societies that
never jointly meet.

Item: The editor of a journal in biology says he expects to understand
about 50 percent of the articles he publishes, and, he adds: "I work
harder at that task than most of my colleagues." The editor of a
chemistry journal [says he] understands fifty to eighty percent of
the articles he chooses to publish, but he "gets" hardly anything
in most of the neighboring chemistry journals.[18]

The unseemly sprawl of the Modern Language Association is notorious, and those of us in religious studies must feel a wry "shock of
recognition" when we hear statements such as these from academic
historians:

History is the maverick among disciplines, the misfit, the bull in the china shop. Since everything has a history and history, potentially at least, deals with everything that ever happened in human society, the historian is a kind of licensed rustler who wanders at will across his scholarly neighbors' fields, poaching their stock and purloining their crops and breaking down their hedges. In a very real sense, it is not a discipline at all.[19]

or:

The bad news [in the eighties] was that the American historical profession was fragmented beyond any hope of unification. The good news was that the fragments were doing very well indeed. New fields were being explored in innovative ways; historical works of considerable originality and even brilliance appeared every year. Among subcommittees of historians there were higher levels of fruitful interaction and higher critical standards than at any time in the past....At the level of everyday practice, things had never been better. One thing the American historical community could not do was sustain a disciplinewide discussion on the meaning of the historical venture as a whole....Discourse across the discipline had effectively collapsed.[20]

I do not rehearse these anecdotes (which are but a few from a collection whose name is Legion) in order to comfort us: "See...they can't figure themselves out either." Rather, I intend them by way of a challenge. For, despite the chaos of particular clarities in the wider world of professional associations, there *are* connections. I have spent some time since being asked to make this presentation reading through the proceedings of various learned societies and speaking with a number of their officers. What has emerged is at least three areas of common concern and discourse which give them a functional (although surely not a substantive) unity. Moreover, each of these three areas connects the insular work of a particular association with a different, wider audience.

The first of these is *theory*. Despite our apparent assent to the proposition enunciated in one of Rudyard Kipling's *Plain Tales*, "Theory killed him dead," most learned societies have found sustained public attention to matters of theory to be both necessary and enlivening. To the degree that theory is a second-order discourse, it provides us with the possibility of meta-languages which give grounds for the attempt to negotiate across

fragmentation in language intelligible to both ourselves and to other intellectual fields of inquiry, thus strengthening internal coherence as well as
connections to the wider academy.

It is not the possibility of unity that I want to stress today, but rather
the relationship of theory to argument and contestation. A philosopher of
science writes:

> In the absence of a paradigm, or some candidate for paradigm,
> all of the facts that could possibly pertain to the development of a
> given science are likely to seem equally relevant.... In the absence
> of a reason for seeking some particular form of more recondite
> information, early fact gathering is restricted to the wealth of
> data that lie ready to hand.... This is the situation that creates the
> schools characteristic of the early stage of a science's development.
> No natural history can be interpreted in the absence of at least
> some implicit body of intertwined theoretical and methodological
> belief that permits selection, evaluation and criticism. [Lacking an
> internal paradigm], it must be externally supplied, perhaps by a
> current metaphysic, by another science, or by personal or historical
> accident.[21]

While two leading students of the human sciences observe:

> Many of the problems of the social sciences are due to the lack of
> effective "disputatious" communities of scholars, who challenge
> each other's specific truth claims with cross-validation and critical
> argument. Too many schools of thought are engaged in produc-
> ing "illustrations" rather than evidence for assertions of descriptive
> facts and theoretical interpretations.[22]

That is to say, the most important function of theory for an academy
such as ours is to force an answer to that most blunt of all questions: "So
what?" Too much of what we do (especially in the format of our meetings) may be placed somewhere between show-and-tell and paraphrase.
Having persuaded ourselves that, whatever else it is, religion is ultimately
important (or, important because it is ultimate), we illicitly use that claim
to justify anything we happen to study as being self-evidently significant.[23] But significance is not a matter of peacock-like self- display, nor is it
guaranteed by something merely being "there." Theory and its attendant

operations (such as comparison) are disciplined exaggerations in the service of knowledge. They provide both the grounds and the means by which *we* re-vision phenomena as *our* data, as significant in that they address *our* theoretical problems. Contestation arises over competing claims to comprehend the *same* data, an argument that, therefore, can never be settled at the level of data. The parataxis of illustrations, of reports on whatever happens to be at hand—"and then..." "and then..."—without ever forcing confrontation that characterizes so many of our sections results in a comity appropriate to a club, but incongruous within an academy.

It is not that we lack theoretical resources. Our AAR colleagues in theology and biblical studies have demonstrated that disciplined arguments between rival constructions of stipulated, shared data are possible and desirable. Stunning, as well as stunningly different, theoretical works continue to be produced by individual members of the AAR— works such as Wayne Proudfoot's *Religious Experience* (1985), J. Samuel Preus's *Explaining Religion* (1987), Hans Penner's *Impasse and Resolution: A Critique of the Study of Religion* (1989), and Peter Homans' *The Ability to Mourn* (1989)[24]—but they are not produced out of the AAR, nor, save for the occasional award or session, have they received sustained critical attention within the AAR.

The second element is *education*. Attention to discourse on education, to questions of theory, method, and practice, is a central matter of persistent concern in most professional associations. In some, presidential addresses routinely focus on some aspect of education. Many learned societies, in both the natural and the human sciences, have, alongside their research journal, a second journal or newsletter wholly devoted to teaching. Committees and commissions on educational affairs abound, and they have frequently been the source of proposals and the site of controversies that have engaged the attention and energy of the entire profession. For many associations, because their subject matter is taught in secondary, collegiate, and graduate schooling, there is a wide range to their concerns, from grade school textbooks to advanced certification.

I am sensible of a considerable irony in commending this topic to you. After all, unique among learned society publications, *JAAR* is not classified by the Library of Congress along with other general publications in its field. *JAAR* is not to be found in "BL" alongside other broadly based journals in religious studies, but rather under the classification, "LC 351," which denotes, "Education/Christian Education/Education Under Church Control."[25] This is in deference to our organizational history. In the past, our ancestor, the

National Association of Biblical Instructors, distinguished itself from the Society of Biblical Literature and Exegesis on the grounds that the

> SBL has for its primary object technical and creative research...,
> NABI has a mission of its own, to it fall matters relating to peda-
> gogy and education. It deals with methods and contents of courses
> of study, and the application of religion to character building.[26]

When NABI was reconfigured as the AAR, interest in the Bible was maintained, the priority of research was newly affirmed,[27] while pedagogy was largely left behind.

It has been good to see, in recent years, a number of harbingers of its return. The Education Committee has been revitalized. The section on the Academic Study of Religion is more focused. *JAAR* has published on pedagogy and religious studies in secondary schools. The inaugural issue of the *Critical Review of Books in Religion* concentrated on textbook review. The AAR is participating, as one of a dozen learned societies, in the Association of American Colleges' inquiry into "study in depth." And, most exciting of all, since our Boston meeting three years ago, there has been increased attention to the study of religion in the public schools, cul-minating in this year's general session.

Beyond the claims of professional responsibility, educational discourse and debate, when moved to the center of a professional society's concerns, are prime modes of fashioning connections. While the rule of proliferation seems to govern the research activities and intellectual interests of any group of scholars (an obedience, in even the most aggressively secular field, to the first commandment in the Hebrew Bible, "Be fruitful and multiply"), the rule of parsimony remains regnant with regard to curricula. Limited by rigid temporal constraints, in this area our expertise is best exhibited in the making of hard choices, in the continual (and sometimes fierce) debates over the "knowledge most worth having." As it joins these issues collectively, a field begins to define its core and forge its canon. Within religious studies, there is no more appropriate public forum for this process than the AAR.

The third element is *public discourse*, where the academic society, act-ing, properly, as a special interest group, brings its particular resources and viewpoints to bear on matters of public policy and concern within the wider civic realm. This is commonplace in other professional associations, and I applaud Jim Wiggins's initiative, this summer, in circulating to the membership a letter concerning the Helms amendment; Jorunn Buckley's organization of a general session, during this meeting, on Rushdie; and Martin Marty's continued efforts to better relate the AAR to the press. But, we need to do more, and we need to do it as a corporate body.

It is fantastic to me that our field, which might be said to "own" the question of canon formation, and which has been deeply involved in teaching and studying *both* the Western classics and the cultural creations of "other" folk for longer than any other field within the contemporary academy, should have conceded, by its conspicuous silence, any role as an informing agent concerning this cluster of controversial issues to adjacent professional societies.

It is distressing to me that this year we have agonized as a nation over questions of desecration, sacrilege, and blasphemy (in literature, in art, and with respect to public symbols such as the flag) without the benefit of substantial input from the one field of study professionally charged with expertise in such matters.

It is outrageous to me that, as the American Academy of *Religion*, we have been collectively silent as the U.S. Supreme Court continues to apply an inadequate and outmoded eighteenth-century *philosophe*'s definition of religion as coercive dogma to recklessly categorize this or that symbol or activity as being "religious" or "secular." However, it is clear that before we talk to and with the public, we need, at our annual meetings, to practice speaking and arguing with each other about such matters, in a way that, shunning univocality, aims, nevertheless, at displaying and clarifying informed choices.

I conclude this attempt to sketch a possible view of our connections with the hope (not limited to the surreal location of this year's convention[28]) that our annual meetings continue as well to express (carnival-like) not only the seriousness of our enterprise but also the "collective effervescence" of our engaging it together, that we demonstrate, again, in the wonderful phrase of Peter Homans (writing on Freud and Weber) that religion can be "an object for the enjoyment of theoretical curiosity."[29]

Notes

Journal of the American Academy of Religion 58, no. 1 (Spring 1990): 1–15. Reprinted by permission of Oxford University Press.

1. James Burke, *Connections* (Boston: Little, Brown, 1978), 287–291.
2. Dwight Beck et al., "Report of the NABI Self-Study Committee," *Journal of Bible and Religion* 32, no. 2 (April 1964): 200.

3. Chester Warren Quimby, "The Word of God: President's Address," *Journal of the National Association of Biblical Instructors* 1, no. 1 (1933): 1.

4. Quoted in Leo O'Donovan, "Going and Coming: The Agenda of an Anniversary," in *Trajectories in the Study of Religion: Addresses at the Seventy-Fifth Anniversary of the American Academy of Religion*, ed. Ray L. Hart (Atlanta: Scholars Press, 1987), 311.

5. Jonathan Z. Smith, general editor, *HarperCollins Dictionary of Religion* (San Francisco: HarperSanFrancisco, 1995); Paul J. Achtemeier, general editor, *Harper's Bible Dictionary* (San Francisco: Harper & Row, 1985).

6. Achtemeier, *Harper's Bible Dictionary*, xx, emphases added.

7. William Scott Green, "Something Strange, Yet Nothing New: Religion in the Secular Curriculum," *Soundings* 71, no. 2/3 (Summer/Fall 1988): 278.

8. Jerome S. Bruner, *Actual Minds, Possible Worlds* (Cambridge, MA: Harvard University Press, 1986), 122–123.

9. Richard Rorty, "Solidarity or Objectivity?" in *Post-Analytic Philosophy*, ed. John Rajchman and Cornel West (New York: Columbia University Press, 1985), 3–19.

10. See the AAR's mission statement as contained in the program book for the 1968 annual meeting, October 17–20, page 5: "It is the aim of the Academy to function as a meeting place where the study of religion in its broadest dimension may be fostered. The establishment of permanent Sections of the Academy, devoted to specific fields, disciplines or subjects within the study of religion [is intended] to strengthen the Academy's role as such a meeting place. [!] Chairmen of the Sections...provide leadership for groups *naturally taking shape* within the Academy along disciplinary...lines" (emphasis added).

11. Beck et al., "Report of the NABI Self-Study Committee," 200; Clyde A. Holbrook, "Why an Academy of Religion?" *Journal of Bible and Religion* 32, no. 2 (April 1964): 103–104.

12. Anonymous, "Editorial Preface," *Journal of Bible and Religion* 33, no. 1 (Jan. 1965): 4.

13. Alvin Toffler, *The Third Wave* (New York: Morrow, 1980), 113, emphases original.

14. On the intellectual incoherence and political threat of departments, and related matters, see also "Religious Studies: Whither (Wither) and Why?" 69 passim; "'Religion' and 'Religious Studies': No Difference At All," 81–82; "Re-Forming the Undergraduate Curriculum," 107–108; and "Why the College Major?" 113–14.—Ed.

15. John Higham, "Paleface and Redskin in American Historiography: A Comment," *Journal of Interdisciplinary History* 16, no. 1 (Summer 1985): 112.

16. Compare the description of meetings of the American Historical Association in Peter Novick, *That Noble Dream: The "Objectivity Question" and the American Historical Profession* (Cambridge: Cambridge University Press, 1988), 580 n. 8.

17. Novick, *Noble Dream*; Mary O. Furner, *Advocacy and Objectivity: A Crisis in the Professionalization of American Social Science, 1865–1905* (Lexington: University Press of Kentucky, 1975).

18. Wayne Booth, "The Idea of a University as Seen by a Rhetorician," *University of Chicago Record* 23, no. 1 (1988): 2.

19. Harold Perkin, "The Historical Perspective," in *Perspectives on Higher Education: Eight Disciplinary and Comparative Views*, ed. Burton R. Clark (Berkeley: University of California Press, 1984), 17–18.

20. Novick, *Noble Dream*, 592.

21. Thomas S. Kuhn, *The Structure of Scientific Revolutions*, 2nd ed. (Chicago: University of Chicago Press, 1970), 15–17.

22. Donald W. Fiske and Richard A. Shweder, eds., "Introduction," *Metatheory in Social Science: Pluralisms and Subjectivities* (Chicago: University of Chicago Press, 1986), 9.

23. On the temptation of self-evident significance, see also "To Double Business Bound," 151.—Ed.

24. Wayne Proudfoot, *Religious Experience* (Berkeley: University of California Press, 1985); J. Samuel Preus, *Explaining Religion: Criticism and Theory from Bodin to Freud* (New Haven, CT: Yale University Press, 1987); Hans Penner, *Impasse and Resolution: A Critique of the Study of Religion* (New York: P. Lang, 1989); Peter Homans, *The Ability to Mourn: Disillusionment and the Social Origins of Psychoanalysis* (Chicago: University of Chicago Press, 1989).

25. Library of Congress, *Classification Outline*, 3rd ed. (Washington, D.C.: Library of Congress, 1975), 11. Library of Congress, *Classification Class L: Education* (Washington, D.C.: Library of Congress, 1984), 138.

26. Ismar J. Peritz, "The National Association of Biblical Instructors and the Society of Biblical Literature and Exegesis," *Journal of the National Association of Biblical Instructors* 1, no. 2 (1933): 29.

27. See Holbrook, "Why an Academy of Religion?"

28. The meeting was held at Disneyland.—Ed.

29. Homans, *Ability to Mourn*, 339.

6

Religious Studies: Whither
(Wither) and Why?

WHEN I BEGAN as a teaching assistant some years ago, a senior professor offered the advice, "Studies of religion will flourish so long as they continue to stand on the body of divinity." The image this conjured in my mind was striking, some Christian version of a Purusha-type primordial sacrifice, and though I was disappointed to learn, after some days of diligent and discrete inquiry, that the phrase was, in fact, a somewhat archaic way of denoting the traditional Protestant divinity school curriculum leading to the bachelor of divinity degree, the phrase has stuck. Indeed, there are even times when, surveying the current scene, I regretfully entertain the fleeting and unlikely suspicion that it might be so. For the warning posed an issue, fiercely fought in the 1960s, expressed as a choice between seminary studies and university studies, between the teaching *of* and the teaching *about* religion, between theological and religious studies. I have a good part of a bookcase in my office filled with publications devoted to such choices, all with respect to a single context: the teaching of religion in a state (public) university. It is a debate, a context, and a history that subsequent generations of teachers in the field are the poorer for not engaging with. It is a debate, a context, and a history that stands behind each of the case studies before us.

1. Initial Generalizations

This autobiographical reminiscence serves as a sign of that history, and it does so to make a point.[1] First, the distinctively North American character of the enterprise: a new market opened up, fueled by an ambiguous and irrelevant judicial aside which gave warrant to what was already in the air, the moving of the study of religion into the tax-supported, public sphere, and the possibility of the gainful employment of individuals capable of engineering such a move. If there were theoretical justifications to be made, they would come later. (We are still waiting.) All that initially mattered was rhetoric and, above all, retooling. To advance this enterprise, changing the character of the training and licensing procedures took priority. No longer would the B.D. be the prerequisite for going on to the M.A. and Ph.D. in religion. It was this shift to which my old professor was reacting. With the benefit of nearly four decades of hindsight, it is possible to rephrase his foreboding and the dichotomies that animated those early discussions with more precision. The field made a decision to give up a (limited) coherence for a (limitless) incoherence. The Protestant seminary curriculum, for all of its inadequacies, constituted a general education in theological studies;[2] religious studies, whether at the collegiate or graduate level, has been unable to construct a general education in religion. Increasingly, this has become an object of pride rather than regret.

The six case studies we have before us illustrate,[3] to varying degrees, some of the consequences of our history as hinted at above.[4] Each does more, in its own fashion, and that is what makes them such interesting reading. These studies invite some concluding generalizations; hence this essay. But generalizations are not easy to come by. The overwhelming impression, on reading these case studies, is one of the diversity of institutional environments in which religious studies needs to find (or, fails at finding) its quite particular niche. These are essays in microecology, and for that reason, in each case, the history of the program has been impossible to narrate without a history of the larger institution.

This preliminary observation, scarcely surprising when one thinks of the diversities within higher education in North America, entails two consequences. First, it suggests a failure of imagination in our field's initial discussions where the public, "secular" university as a new setting for the academic study of religion was far too readily thought of as essentially homogenous space. Second, and of more gravity, it reminds us that localism abounds. Localism is characteristic of almost every field of learning. It is precisely the task of professionalism to serve as a crosscutting impulse towards suprainstitutional standardization. (I employ the term "impulse" because the tension is, with the rarest of exceptions, never resolved.) Our professional associations appear to have chosen (this may be too deliberate a term) to foster localisms of every stripe, thus undercutting the very function that requires their existence.[5]

There are two other initial generalizations that might be made on the basis of these six case studies, neither of which is peculiar to religious studies, but both of which appear to take odd and unfortunate twists when applied to the field: economic forces and personality clashes.

Religious studies came into being in its present ubiquitous form during the academic boom years of the mid-1960s through the 1970s. (Fueled as well, as Walter Capps has persistently and correctly reminded us, by the special environment created by the Vietnam War.) It is therefore of no surprise that it becomes particularly vulnerable when that boom goes bust. This is the scarcely disguised message of the case studies: when times are more stringent, a new program, added when times were more generous, comes under special scrutiny and appears to be, *prima facie*, a candidate for reduction, dispersion, or termination. Nothing special here. And yet, with rare exception (Arizona State), the programs that serve as our examples seemed incapable of mounting a counter campaign. While there are several reasons for this, one stands out. By and large, religious studies lacks a constituency. Based on these studies, and setting aside self-serving rhetoric about secularism, this lack has its origin in the nature of the teaching enterprise and in the self-definition of the field. It is clear from the case studies, and from other data as well,[6] that courses in religious studies largely function as "service courses" (a despicable term, which remains, in this instance, useful for designating the fact that the majority of enrollments in religion courses are one-time electives, either fulfilling some distribution requirement or meeting a student's interest). Few programs in religious studies have numbers of majors commensurate with their enrollments; few majors go on to graduate studies in religion. This pattern serves to maintain a self-fulfilling prophecy. If there are few majors, then each course is, to a large degree, an introductory course, making it unattractive to potential majors. (I might add, that this well-known fact, despite our pretensions to the contrary, that religious studies is largely an elective part of collegiate education and not an affair of majors or graduate students, makes utterly irresponsible the field's widespread failure to undertake serious constructions of general education programs in religion.) Faced with economic stringencies, this failure to create a strong campus constituency is fatal, robbing religious studies of the only effective voice, in hard times, against the wider faculty's myopic "your-program-at-the-expense-of-mine" mentality. The one-time-only enrollment pattern not only fails to produce such a voice, it fosters the personalism endemic to religious studies programs (and to the study of religion). It is almost impossible to translate affection for Professor X's class into support for the department of which Professor X is a member.

This is compounded by religious studies' own deep unease with its "prehistory," that makes it nervous about appealing to some off-campus constituencies, namely organized, local religious groups. Its public rhetoric (the facts, of course, may be quite otherwise) is one of distance, of the study of religion from afar, and the price for that stance is paid when religious studies needs outside allies. Furthermore, despite the apparent "success" in the case of the University of Pennsylvania, the professional associations in religious studies, because of their general inability to adopt that public voice characteristic of professional associations, have not proven to be effective off-campus allies.[7]

In making its case in times of budgetary scrutiny, religious studies is often left with the weakest supporting evidence of all: enrollment figures. Always an insufficient rationale for a program, the inherent weakness of enrollment statistics is compounded when Newton's law begins to make itself felt, that which goes up must eventually come down. Demographics are two-edged weapons, as many programs have come to learn.

I found the personality clashes which formed a subtext to many of the case narratives disturbing. Not that such clashes are in themselves surprising. After all, colleges and universities annually spend large sums to add new, cantankerous, social odd-bodies to their faculties—guaranteed to be so only after extensive national searches. What is troubling is that there is no apparent second-order language to mitigate, to negotiate, the debates left unresolved since our birth: e.g., religion/religions, religion from afar/religion from up close. Lacking such theoretical and professional discourse, there remain only personalities and their alliances, the latter undercutting any attempt at creating a general constituency.

Three of the institutional histories (quite by accident, all Canadian) seemed especially prey to the issues of economy, demography, constituency, and personality, in the latter case, being unable to find an institutionally secure way of "teaching our differences" (to use a term popularized by Gerald Graff). This was compounded (as it was also at the University of Pennsylvania) by an extraordinary series of botched administrative procedures and failures to extend common courtesies, along with a surprising lack of candor and consultation on the part of administrative officials. Arizona State, by contrast, seems an exemplary model of how to make these very same issues work to the program's advantage.

2. *Problems of Our Own Design*

Having written this much by way of the most general generalizations out of the six case studies, I wish to lift up one of them for particular attention: the University of Pennsylvania.

If 1963, the year of the U.S. Supreme Court decision on *School District of Abington v. Schempp* (374 U.S. 203) marks the mythical year of the founding of the present state of religious studies in the United States, then some apocalyptic-minded mythographer may yet point to 1993 as the year of the portent of its demise. It was a year that a new, not yet acculturated administrator inquired after the haberdashery of the emperor of religious studies and drew the thoroughly appropriate conclusion: rather than new clothing, the field seemed to be both naked and uncommonly unashamed.

The University of Pennsylvania, through the efforts of Claude Welch, played, in the 1960s, an ancestral role in the foundation myth of the new religious studies. In the 1990s, it provides the *locus classicus* of the present state of the field, illustrating more of a muddle than a model. Its difficulties are not an example of the parlous state of focus on religion in an increasingly secular (it is not) age, but rather are entirely of our own design.

Let me return for a moment to where I began, with the attempt to transubstantiate the "body of divinity." I observed then that three important preconditions had not been met: theory, general studies, and professionalism.[8] This is not entirely accurate. The crafting of a pseudomeeting of these preconditions has been the labor of the last decades. In a wholly understandable overreaction against the well-meaning, endlessly tolerant amateurs who often comprised religion programs prior to the 1960s, a new set of standards was forged: competence in a particular religious tradition measured largely by the acquisition of philological expertise accompanied by an emergent ethic of particularity which suggested that any attempt at generalization violated the personhood of those studied. Lip service might be paid to more general issues, but only in the most introductory courses, never to be employed again.[9] The question of what constituted competency or training in generalization was ignored; generalization was reduced to the status of an avocation. Graduate training in religion became chiefly a matter of linguistic expertise (largely farmed out to other departments) and the attaining of methods from the human sciences appropriate to the study of particular cultures (largely developed by, and often taught better in, other departments).[10] All other levels of the system, from the increasing Balkanization of the AAR to the ethos of coverage in collegiate programs, followed suit.

The 1993 crisis at the University of Pennsylvania put the question in an inescapable manner. If the adjective (a particular religious tradition) rather than the noun (religion) has priority in your studies, if your prime competence is certified by another department, what is it that you do that you cannot do in another location?[11] If the constituent parts of religious studies are area studies, why should the amalgam not be disassembled and the parts returned to their respective wholes? Or to put this another way, from a dean's perspective: would the area programs be more enhanced by the presence of individuals committed to the study of religion in that region than religious studies would be enhanced by the presence of those same individuals committed to the study of religion in particular areas if the program in religious studies is not prepared to insist, in some explicit and coherent fashion, on the priority of some generic category of religion?

The appropriate analogy, I would think, is languages. Most individuals interested in particular languages or families of languages find their homes in area programs (whether geographically or linguistically named). Most individuals interested in language itself (regardless of their competence in particular languages) find their home in linguistics departments. Each may find the status of the other a provocative issue for theoretical (and political) discourse. But, the division of labor is clear, even if blurred (through joint appointments and the like) in practice.[12]

One can read with great care, and collegial good will, the statement from the University of Pennsylvania. One will not find a single sentence in it that provides a warrant for its repeated claim that there is an autonomous field of the study of religion "on its own terms, as its own discipline...as its own field of study" (388). There is no referent for the possessive pronoun except the reiterated appeal to a universal (or, at least, ubiquitous) sense of humans being "religious"—whatever that might mean in this context. The closest to a definition that I could find is the phrase, the "deepest issues that concern them" (391), at best a weak version of the poorly constructed Tillichian formulation.[13]

The demise of the religious studies program at University of California, Santa Cruz, presents a parallel set of issues, explicitly recognized in Gary Lease's account where he put the matter with precision:

> You cannot, in the long run, have it both ways: One cannot claim to be a discipline and yet not draw the consequences, i.e., claim such an identity and nevertheless not express it curricularly. For curriculum is the *identity expression* of a discipline....[A] claimed

identity without any content or substance, as was the case with the
Religious Studies program, is no identity at all, and must finally
lead to dissolution. (322, emphasis added)

Whether his proposed solution, that religious studies find a role as an
aspect of what is essentially a (graduate) cultural studies program, is the
solution—in quite different form, also the solution adopted by Alberta—
remains *sub judice*. But it is a responsible proposal in that it accepts fully
the consequences of his strictures on the term "religion."

3. *Conclusion*

If there is a moral to these case studies, it is surely that merely pointing to
some distribution map is not an effective way of establishing the topography
of a field of study; that despite genuine disagreements, such a topography
can only be achieved by collaborative work, work which is represented and
exemplified at every level of the curriculum; that religious studies has focus,
if it has focus at all, only at the second-order level of theoretical discourse and
not at the primary level of facts and ad hoc typologizations. It is only theories and concepts that convert facts into data, that render them significant as
examples of larger intellectual issues which comprise the agendum, debated
though it may be, of a field. The observation by Alec Vidler made during the
British debate over divinity faculties/religious studies faculties in the 1960s,
a debate carried out on quite different presuppositions than that which animated the North American controversies, nevertheless still holds:

> There is room for doubt about what exactly "religion" means in this
> context (obviously it does not mean [only] Christianity). However it
> is to be interpreted, it is manifestly a respectable academic title for
> something. One of the tasks of a department of religious studies
> would be to inquire what it does or ought to mean as an essential
> academic concern.[14]

Notes

Method and Theory in the Study of Religion 7, no. 4 (1995): 407–414. Reprinted
by permission.

1. Compare the next pages with "Here and Now: Prospects for Graduate
    Education," 42–46.—Ed.

2. I do not mean to suggest that the traditional seminary curriculum was always a model of coherence. What focus it had has been much dissipated in recent years. See Edward Farley, *Theologia: The Fragmentation and Unity of Theological Education* (Philadelphia: Fortress Press, 1983).

3. The volume of *MTSR* in which this essay appeared as an afterword was devoted to six case studies on the rise—and in most cases, decline—of religious studies programs at North American universities. The volume was guest edited by Gary Lease, who (in his own words) was sometimes seen as the "killer" of the program at the University of California, Santa Cruz. Parenthetical page references are to this volume, whose table of contents is as follows:

    Gary Lease, "Foreword," 299–303.

    ———, "The Rise and Fall of Religious Studies at Santa Cruz: A Case Study in Pathology, or the *Rest of the Story*," 305–324.

    Marilyn Nefsky, "The Rise and Fall of Religious Studies at the University of Lethbridge," 325–339.

    Eva Neumaier-Dargyay, "The Department of Religious Studies at the University of Alberta: An Account of a Restructuring Process, 1993–1994," 341–349.

    Donald Wiebe, "Alive, but Only Barely: Graduate Studies in Religion at the University of Toronto," 351–381.

    E. Ann Matter, "The Academic Culture of Disbelief: Religious Studies at the University of Pennsylvania," 383–392.

    Linell E. Cady, "Religious Studies and the Public University: A Case Study at Arizona State University," 393–406.

    In his foreword, Lease writes, "As Jonathan Z. Smith opined on first seeing the essays collected here, they read like an obituary.... What's the count? Of the six programmes chosen for exposure here, three have passed from the scene, either directly or as part of a restructured merger (Santa Cruz, Lethbridge, Alberta); two have survived, in various states of disrepair (Toronto, Pennsylvania); and only one seems to be thriving (Arizona)." Lease asked Smith for "a summary analysis that attempts to identify the most salient issues and future developments," resulting in the present essay.—Ed.

4. I have critically reviewed some of this history in "'Religion' and 'Religious Studies': No Difference at All," 77–90.

5. The most striking sign of the lack of professionalism in these case studies is the insipid or detrimental advice rendered by a succession of "peer review" and advisory committees to the various programs.

6. See, among others, the report by a task force of the American Academy of Religion, "Religion," in the Association of American Colleges Reports from the Field, which forms the second volume of the AAC's *Liberal Learning and the Arts and Sciences Major* (Washington, D.C.: Association of American Colleges, 1990), 169–183.

7. On the issue of the professional association and public voice with respect to the American Academy of Religion, see "Connections," 49–61 [esp. 60–61—Ed.].

8. Compare this list to the three conditions discussed in "Connections," 57–61.—Ed.

9. This can be illustrated by most introductory college-level textbooks which contain an introductory chapter dealing with methods and definitions of religion. On my reading, the issues and problems raised in these first chapters never recur or are alluded to again in the body of the work which continues, unperturbed, to say what it would have said anyway.

10. See the more extensive discussion in "Here and Now: Prospects for Graduate Education," 37–48.—Ed.

11. On the intellectual incoherence and political threat of departments, and related matters, see also "Connections," 55; "'Religion' and 'Religious Studies': No Difference At All," 81–82; "Re-Forming the Undergraduate Curriculum," 107–108; and "Why the College Major?" 113–14.—Ed.

12. On my campus, the linguistics professor who happens to know Albanian will have a joint appointment in Balkan Studies and teach the language there. When this is done, it is done with the full knowledge that this is not teaching general linguistics. The professor also tells me that Albanian was learned because of a problem in general language theory. With the exception of Mel Spiro (professionally classified as an anthropologist), I can think of no one in contemporary religious studies who states they chose their particular area of study to solve an issue in the general theoretical construction of religion.

13. I charitably reduce to a footnote one of the rare occurrences of the general noun "religion" in the essay, the obscurantist quotation of C. G. Jung that, in the modern world, "religion can only be replaced by religion" (391).

14. Alec Vidler, "The Future of Divinity," in Crisis in the Humanities, ed. John H. Plumb (Baltimore: Penguin Books, 1964), 92.

7

Are Theological and Religious Studies Compatible?

ONE MIGHT HAVE the initial sense, on reading the question we are here called together to discuss, of "here we go again," admitting, thereby, some degree of fatigue with the issue of the compatibility of theological and religious studies. Alternatively, one might find in the question a perennial problem, the spectre that haunts religious studies, or venture the notion that it is one of the aporiae of our enterprise.

I find myself to be largely of the first persuasion. Neither the article in *Lingua Franca*—an article largely tone deaf to both sides of the argument, missing, thereby, the major issues that do divide us—nor the spin-doctoring in the *New York Times* suggests much freshness to the question.[1] Theological and religious studies are clearly different and can therefore be compared across their differences, thus yielding one form of second-order compatibility, but I doubt that most students in their work-a-day labors find the need to do so.

I do not mean to imply that I do not covet the excuse of the topic as an occasion for celebrating Eric Sharpe. I have always profited from our conversations and learned from reading him. The last time Eric and I shared a platform together was ten years ago in a session of the 1986 Santa Barbara Colloquium, "Religion within the Limits of Reason Alone," where our assigned topic was the same question written differently: "What is the difference between religion and religious studies?"

While I hesitate to speak for Eric Sharpe, I sense in his paper, despite the fascinating details, that he, too, finds some measure of fatigue with the question.[2] Much of his explicit reflection on the matter reduces the issue to departmental demographics and individual relationships. I gain little sense of urgency from these.

As Sharpe, himself, acknowledges with respect to this "hardy perennial subject," this "debate...once occupied a good deal of one's time and energy" even though he now finds it "chastening...to find out how very little real progress seems to have been made since one was involved with it." So I turn, instead, to a work of his where the matter is more heated, his magisterial intellectual biography of Söderblom in which our question was instantiated in the professional life of a single, significant scholar and church leader. I have been much helped by Sharpe's framing of the issue for contemporary scholarship in this work.

Sharpe writes of a "crisis of identity" between the "academic study of religion" and its opposing camp "for which it is hard to find a name." He goes on to provide two names for the "opponent"—a duality I, for one, find provocative of thought. The first is the conventional opponent, the "theological" approach, which he somewhat blandly, though commonsensically, defines as being that which "affirms—or at least does not go out of its way to contradict—some dominant religious tradition." The second kind of opponent he terms the "transcendental approach" defined as that which "attempts to look beyond traditions to some ultimate reality...to look beyond [religious phenomena] to their ultimate significance."[3] I want to suggest that it is this second sort of position, the "transcendental," held both by some theologians and, I suspect, by many more students of religion, that is the tensive position both to theological *and* to religious studies.

I find no problem, in principle, between the "academic study of religion" and the "theological approach" as Sharpe defines it. But this is because I invoke a principle of subordination. After all, individuals who "affirm" (Sharpe's term) some "religious tradition" make up the bulk of the data for the study of religion. Even if the language of affirmation is strengthened, as it surely must be, to something like "articulate the truth claims of some religious tradition within the bounds sanctioned by that tradition," such articulations are still a significant fraction of what we study. (I add that theological studies as well may compare and seek to understand the articulate affirmations both within the diversities of their own tradition and of other traditions.) In what I freely acknowledge to be a necessarily imperializing move, theology is one appropriate object of study for religious studies. From the perspective of the academic study of religion, theology is a datum, the theologian is a native informant.

As I have argued in a variety of contexts, the study of religion is ill-served by the notion of "primordial" (itself, largely an interest of the "transcendental approach"). We need to be far more attentive to the exegetical labors of religious folk, to their systematic projects of articulation and understanding. In the same spirit in which I welcome the study of the totalizing mythic endeavors, the *univers imaginaires*, of an Ogotemmêli or an Antonio Guzmàn,[4] I would hope, some day, to read a consonant treatment of the analogous enterprise of Karl Barth's *Church Dogmatics*.

To repeat: Aside from matters of academic politics, matters largely, though alas not wholly, of the past as religious studies muscled in on turf previously controlled by theological studies, I see in principle no conflict with theology which provides the academic study of religion with those emic, often experience-near, and always community-oriented accounts in historically particularized languages whose description, classification, interpretation, comparison, and explanation constitute the way religious studies earns its daily bread.

The conflict, as I see it, arises almost wholly with the second "opponent" Sharpe names, the "transcendentalists," who propose a powerful, rival understanding of the necessarily plural interpretative and comparative ventures which characterize the study of religion. That is to say, it is a conflict at the same generic level over (at least potentially) the same data.

Unlike the theologians, the "transcendentalists" hold themselves responsible to no particular community. Unlike students of religion, they do not find in their being historically and culturally situated a tool to play across placements of near and far. They do not seek, as both students of religion and, in a different sense, theologians, modes of translation between one language and another—be it natural languages or the artificial languages of scholarship, be it between the constraints of place or time—but rather appear to strive for some Esperanto, in some "transcendentalist" projects, for an odd sort of no-speech which seeks to reduce human language to an inarticulate pointing to someplace else.

While students of religion may employ the generic term "religion," they know full well that there is no one who lives such a "religion," just as there are no *existant genera*. As Steven Katz and others have argued with respect to "mysticism," so too here: language is not a secondary formation, posterior to experience.[5] We do not experience the world independently of the social and conventional ways in which it is represented. Language cannot be precipitated out and leave a remainder. That is to say, the *re* of re-presentation remains always at the level of representation. This is what makes the imagination of the human sciences possible within which the study of religion finds its place, with translation, and its necessary insufficiency, as its primary model.

To refuse this is to hold to the odd sort of tautology that was once claimed by Chicago's History of Religions field: "It is the contention of the discipline of History of Religions that a valid case can be made for the interpretation of transcendence as transcendence"[6]—a quixotic repetition of the notion exemplified by Borges's fictional character Pierre Menard that a word can only be translated by itself.

It is this debate about language and experience, the questions of translation, the controversies as to whether experience can ever be immediate or whether it is always mediated, the issues of contingency and situation that constitute the serious matters that divide us. It is a debate which cannot usefully be reduced to the query as to whether theological and religious studies are compatible.

Notes

Bulletin of the Council of Societies for the Study of Religion 26, no.3 (1997): 60–61. © Equinox Publishing Ltd., 1997. Reprinted by permission.

1. Charlotte Allen, "Is Nothing Sacred?" *Lingua Franca* 6, no. 7 (1996): 30–40. Gustav Niebuhr, "Religion Journal. Finding a Religious Quilt That Is Patchwork," *New York Times*, November 25, 1996: 13.
2. Eric J. Sharpe, "The Compatibility of Theological and Religious Studies: Historical, Theoretical, and Contemporary Perspectives," *Bulletin of the Council of Societies for the Study of Religion* 26, no. 3 (1997): 52–59.
3. Eric J. Sharpe, *Nathan Söderblom and the Study of Religion* (Chapel Hill: University of North Carolina Press, 1990), xxi.
4. Marcel Griaule, *Conversations with Ogotemmêli: An Introduction to Dogon Religious Ideas* (London: Oxford University Press, 1965). Gerardo Reichel-Dolmatoff, *Amazonian Cosmos* (Chicago: University of Chicago Press, 1971).
5. Steven T. Katz, ed., *Mysticism and Religious Traditions* (New York: Oxford University Press, 1983).
6. *Announcements: The Divinity School, University of Chicago* (1960–1961): 3.

8

"Religion" and "Religious Studies":
No Difference at All

FROM ONE PERSPECTIVE, if I take seriously the title for this session which has embedded within it the question we are to discuss, it will not take me very long to transact my part of the business. "What is the difference between religion and religious studies?" Either every difference or no difference at all. "What is the difference between religious studies and other humanistic and social scientific fields?" In principle, none.

I have given two opposing answers to the first question—that of the difference between religion and religious studies—because I know what is usually meant by such a question (for which, the approved answer would be, "every difference"), and I know how I would like to take the question (under this guise, the answer I have proposed elsewhere would be, "no difference at all").

As usually understood, the distinction between religion and religious studies reduces to some version of the duality between "being religious" or "doing religion" and the study of the same. This sort of distinction is expressed in our conference document by the disclaimer, "the academic study of religion is clearly not itself religious."[1] It is a preeminently political contrast, one of value in carving out a place for the study of religion within the university, but of dubious value beyond. It is, quite frankly, a ploy. We signal this political ancestry by using as contrast terms, "seminary," or "theological," or by adopting the valorizing terminology of the academy: first, *history (Geschichte)* or *science (Wissenschaft)*, more recently, and happily free from Teutonic pedigree, *studies*. The elaboration of the distinction has set the political (and secondarily, the intellectual) agenda of religious studies in the last century as signaled in your conference document with the phrase, "it was clearly recognized at Santa Barbara that

the task was to develop the academic study of religion in a manner appropriate to the letters and science mission of a modern, secular state university." Note which party conforms "in a manner appropriate" to whom. The
political distinction was, at heart, a counsel to passivity and integration,
not to interesting thought.

As a sheerly political move, analogous to other self-justifications from
other fields who sought recognition and legitimation from centers of articulate power, the distinction can be applauded. Raised to the level of theory, it has proved mischievous, especially when confused with other sorts
of distinctions such as those between the "insider" and the "outsider"—
the "emic" and the "etic" in contemporary jargon. Its most current formulation is that between the normative and the descriptive.

While I recognize the value of this distinction in some analytic contexts, as used in religious studies it appears all too often to be a continu-
ation of the old political jargon (after many of the battles have been long
settled). It does not yield the same sort of theoretical clarification that
analogous distinctions provide: for example, as between the formal and
the empirical, the monothetic and the polythetic, definition and classification. It continues to serve the old tactical ends of establishing legitimacy by lay, juridical language rather than theoretical discourse. It is
but a more elegant form of the sort of language employed by the French
Ministry of Education in 1885 (as Eric Sharpe reminds us) when it closed
down the Catholic Theological Faculties and established the Fifth Section
of Religious Sciences: "we do not wish to see the cultivation of polemics
but of critical research, we wish to see the examination of texts and not
the discussion of dogmas."[2] This language was continued by the United
States Supreme Court, in *School District of Abington v. Schempp* (374 U.S.
203 (1963)), when Mr. Justice Goldberg declared, in what was to be the
"Magna Carta" for religious studies within state universities: "It seems
clear to me...that the Court would recognize the propriety of...the teaching *about* religion as distinguished from the teaching *of* religion in the
public schools."[3]

Not only is the putative distinction naive and political, it is also anach-
ronistic. It speaks out of a period when the norms of theological inquiry
(as experienced in the West) were largely governed by an intact canon,
when the ideology of the human sciences were chiefly governed by the
goal of achieving "objectivity" or "value-free" knowledge. The most superficial reading of much contemporary theological discourse will reveal that
the notion of an intact canon has largely been abandoned or has been

perceived as problematic. An equally superficial reading of the current literature of human sciences will reveal that the subjectivity of the individual researcher now stands at the very center of the critical enterprise. Kant, Marx, Freud, et al., have won over both sides. Within the academy, neither can escape the discourse of modernity.

Allow me to introduce a revision of the question by taking a bit of a detour, a set of reflections first stimulated by a project undertaken by Walter Capps at UCSB at least a decade ago. He convened a conference to study the "the undeniable fact that religious studies may have created a phenomenon against which it has been judiciously trying to distinguish itself. Religious studies, in effect, has stimulated religion." But, what a religion! For it has been, more often than not, one shorn of most if not all communal and consensual sanctions. We have seen the emergence, within the academy, of a highly personalist religiosity in which each individual constitutes his or her own ad hoc canon in the name of generic religion. (In Burckhardt's sense of the term, what we have seen is the emergence of a kind of religious "barbarism.") This generic term "religion" requires further attention.

I take it we can agree that the term "religion" is not an empirical category. It is a second-order abstraction. This changes our previous mode of discourse. While it is possible to speak of theorizing about religion in general, it is impossible to "do it" or "believe it" or be normative or descriptive with respect to it. Ways of meaningful speaking of first-order phenomena have become impossibly conjoined to a second-order abstraction resulting, at the very least, in misplaced concreteness. What meaning, then, can the word "religion" have in such a situation?

College catalogs and college-level textbooks display two chief understandings.[4] The first employs the language of *religion* and postulates some essence of religion (usually vaguely defined in terms of ultimacy or transcendence) which becomes manifest in particular historical or geographical traditions or artifacts. However, the mechanism of the "manifestation" is rarely exhibited, and the ubiquity of the alleged essence is not much insisted on after the opening chapter or first lecture in the introductory course.

The second employs the language of the *religious*. It appears to make the claim that there is a religious aspect, approach, perspective, or dimension to some subject or area of human experience which has nonreligious dimensions as well. As in the first case, the definition of the "religious" in such formulations is vague. The "religious" most frequently appears to function as a sort of extra-plus (the "most integrative" is quite common). Here the "religious" has come to mean some loosely characterized quality of life or experience.

It is we, that is to say, the academy, who fill these definitions with content or meaning, who give them status, who employ them as part of our language. It is we in the academy who imagine kingdoms, phyla, classes, orders, families, and genera—life, after all, is lived only at the level of species or individuals. As Herb Fingarette wrote on another topic some years ago: "Home is always home for someone.... There is no absolute home in general."[5] *Mutatis mutandis* religion in general.

This has led me to the relatively simple proposition that it is the study of religion that created the category, it is the study of religion that invented "religion." As I have written elsewhere:

> If we have correctly understood the archeological and textual record, man has had his entire history in which to imagine deities and modes of interaction with them. But man, more precisely Western man, has had only the last few centuries in which to imagine religion. It is this act of second-order, reflexive imagination which must be the central preoccupation of any student of religion. That is to say, while there is a staggering amount of data, of phenomena, of human experiences and expressions that might be characterized in one culture or another, by one criterion or another as religious—there is no data for religion. Religion is solely the creation of the scholar's study. It is created for the scholar's analytic purposes by his imaginative acts of comparison and generalization. Religion has no independent existence apart from the academy.[6]

This is to say, the concept "religion" functions as a category formation for religious studies as its close analogue "culture" functions for anthropology or "language" functions for general linguistics. Like them, it is to be judged solely by its theoretical utility.

As an aside I may add that there is no more pathetic spectacle in all of academia than the endless citation of the little list of fifty-odd definitions of religion from James Leuba's *Psychology of Religion* in introductory textbooks as proof that religion is beyond definition, that it is fundamentally a *mysterium*. Nonsense! We created it and, following the Frankenstein-ethos, we must take responsibility for it.

I doubt, factually, that religious studies constitutes a "coherent disciplinary matrix in and of itself." I equally doubt that we should attempt to make the claim. It is, once again, an enterprise that served well the politics of establishing departments by some principle of intellectual economy. It is an enterprise that characterized nineteenth-century encyclopedia and philosophical classifications of the sciences,[7] but I know of no other field preoccupied with making such claims at the present time.[8] The question of distinction between fields of study in the academy has largely yielded to the complex question of the classification of objects of study within broad domains of inquiry. There is, most certainly, no "unique idiom or language of religious studies"...not even a dialect, at best, only a mongrel, polyglot jargon, again quite typical of the present academy. We are, at our firmest, what Stephen Toulmin has termed a "would-be discipline," and we must be content, for the present, that that be the case.[9] After all, the same characterization applies to the vast majority of our conversation partners within the academy in both the humanities and the social sciences.

Allow me to cite two descriptions of the characteristics of "would-be disciplines." I would hope not only that we would recognize ourselves in these descriptions, but also that they might suggest some curricular implications. The first is from Stephen Toulmin's *Human Understanding*, which remains the most searching discussion of intellectual disciplines and professions that I know.

Toulmin writes:

[Those] attempting to co-operate in launching a new science (say) may not merely disagree about their particular observations and interpretations, concepts and hypotheses: they may even lack common standards for deciding what constitutes a genuine problem, a valid explanation, or a sound theory....the various practitioners of a scientific "would-be discipline" can presuppose no agreed aims, ideals, or standards. The immediate result of this lack is that theoretical debate in the field concerned becomes largely—and unintentionally—methodological or philosophical; inevitably, it is directed less at interpreting particular empirical findings than at debating the general acceptability (or unacceptability) of rival approaches, patterns of explanation, and standards of judgement. [Within a "would-be discipline"] the theoretical debate can—at best—concentrate on the acknowledged methodological failings of the subject in the attempt to analyze, and see the relations between, the alternative intellectual goals which it might be pursuing.[10]

The second quotation is from the initial pages of Thomas Kuhn's opening chapter, "The Route to Normal Knowledge," in *The Structure of Scientific Revolutions*:

> In the absence of a paradigm or some candidate for paradigm, all of the facts that could possibly pertain to the development of a given science are likely to seem equally relevant. As a result, early fact gathering is a far more random activity than the one that subsequent scientific development makes familiar. Furthermore, in the absence of a reason for seeking some particular form of more recondite information, early fact-gathering is restricted to the wealth of data that lie ready to hand....This is the situation that creates the schools characteristic of the early stages of a science's development. No natural history can be interpreted in the absence of at least some implicit body of intertwined theoretical and methodological belief that permits selection, evaluation and criticism. [Lacking internal paradigm] it must be externally supplied, perhaps by a current metaphysic, by another science, or by personal or historical accident. No wonder that in the early stages of development of any science different men confronting the same range of phenomena, but not usually all the same particular phenomena, describe and interpret them in different ways.[11]

In the absence of that corporate consciousness which constitutes an intact discipline, the present task for the student of religion is a kind of "damage control," taking up the various sorts of issues signaled by Toulmin and Kuhn and substituting individual self-consciousness for collective agreement (or stipulation) by making plain that one is engaged in matters of choice rather than happenstance (or, for that matter, revelation). This consciousness must be demanded and trained for at both the levels of data (i.e., examples accepted for purposes of an argument) and of interpretative frameworks. With respect to the one I have argued:

> For the self-conscious student of religion, no datum possesses intrinsic interest. It is of value only insofar as it can serve as an exemplum of some fundamental issue in the imagination of religion. The student of religion must be able to articulate clearly why "this" rather than

"that" was chosen as an exemplum. His primary skill is concentrated in this choice. This effort at articulate choice is all the more difficult, hence all the more necessary, for the student of religion who accepts neither the boundaries of canon nor of community as constituting his intellectual domain, in providing his range of exempla. Implicit in this effort at articulate choice are three conditions. First, that the exemplum has been well and fully understood. This requires the mastery of both the relevant primary material and the history and tradition of its interpretation. Second, that the exemplum be displayed in the service of some important theory, some paradigm, some fundamental question, some central element in the academic imagination of religion. Third, that there be some method for explicitly relating the exemplum to the theory, paradigm, or question and some stipulated method for evaluating each in terms of the other.[12]

With respect to the other, I have argued, with particular reference to graduate studies, that:

whatever else they learn, graduate students should be exposed to their field's past in such a way as to learn the art of critical evaluation and to gain the ability to account for this past in terms of a broadly based historical consciousness. They must learn the context of their second-order tradition as well as they have mastered the primary texts, and the difficult art of evaluating each in terms of the other as well as in terms of historical perspectives and intellectual principles. They should learn, through explicit attention to rules and by the careful study of examples, the crafts of argument and dialectics, the art of making things count and of determining what counts, as well as more philosophical issues relative to the types and status of definitions, taxonomies and explanations. They should be capable of stipulating why their chosen data are exemplary in terms of clearly stated, well-formulated issues central to their academic field, and they should be taught ways of "cost accounting" for the decisions of choice and interpretation that they make. Such concerns (and there are others which might have equal claim to attention) are not the domain of any particular discipline or field of study. They are what constitutes an endeavor as academic. As such, they form the elements of a general education at the graduate level.[13]

This last begins to hint at my reasons for responding to the second question before us, "What is the difference between religious studies and other humanistic and social scientific fields?" with the blunt answer: "In principle, none." That is to say, to the degree that we are citizens of the academy, sharing common presuppositions as to "what is the case" (e.g., the appeal in the conference document to the widely held notion of *homo symbolicus*), our commonalities, qua the academy, far outweigh what I would understand to be differences of economic efficiency that separate the currently mapped fields within the human sciences. From this point of view, I am more than content to hold the position, critically described in Larson's paper, that "the distinction between religious studies and other humanistic disciplines is largely heuristic" and that "religious studies is simply one more functional way of cutting up the pie in the modern university." Nor am I aware of other "would-be disciplines" making stronger claims. The internal differences within one field are often sharper than the extramural differences between one field and another, or, to personalize this, each of us frequently finds closer conversation partners with some representative of "other" fields than we do with the majority of members of our own putative area. What is more, Toulmin, in the passage I quoted, gives us good reason why this is bound to be the case.

I am not in the least persuaded by the conference document's attempt to describe a "second level"; in particular, I am made uneasy by its appeal to "the apprehension or experience of transcendence" as the differentiating principle. Beyond some doubt that a "discipline" is usefully described in terms of subject matter rather than in terms of methods, conventions, and intellectual tasks, there are profound and well-known problems with the formulation which may be expressed briefly in two parallel forms. (1) As I have already indicated, I find the language of transcendence distressingly vague. A field in quest of an undefined (or, is it held to be undefinable?) *sine qua non* is no field at all. (2) Despite its Geertzian flavor, this revision of an essentially Tillichian proposal does not escape the dual problems of pansymbolism and monopolarity which were thoroughly exposed by Charles Hartshorne and taken up by W. M. Urban, W. P. Alston, and H. H. Penner, among others.[14]

Even more troublesome is the derivative proposition in the conference document that religious studies be understood as an "inquiry into the human need for symbolizing transcendence." Unless this be radically reformulated as "an inquiry into the human response to the transcendent"—a move that the document appears properly to eschew—what prevents this statement of "need" from being subsumed by some form of biological, social, or psychological functionalism, with all of the latter's well-known problems, thus collapsing the grounds for the proposed disciplinary distinction? If one rewrites the definition in the conference statement in a manner formally congruent with that by a sophisticated functionalist such as Melford Spiro, the problem for its proposers becomes clear: "Religion is a network of culturally patterned symbols of and interactions with culturally posited modes of transcendence."[15]

I fear such arguments concerning the putative autonomy of religious studies will not rapidly disappear. I must insist that, when not sheerly political, they are not designed to serve an academic end, but to protect the object of religion (the sacred, transcendent, what have you) from the academy by declaring its autonomy—that is to say, a weak return to the old enterprise of Otto. While there have been a few elegant and instructive recent examples of the discourse of autonomy (recall Kurt Rudolph versus Alfred Rupp),[16] most such endeavors have yielded sterile, inedible fruit.

For these and other reasons, I doubt the success of the fissive enterprise, let alone its legitimacy. However, there are other sorts of reasons for abstention from such differentiations which are for me far more provocative.

The first is the sense that we have reached a point in the academy where many of the fields within the human sciences are debating the same issues from quite similar perspectives. What appears to have emerged is a broad agreement upon a number of coequal possibilities which, while surely characteristic of particular scholars or scholarly styles, cannot be used to identify one field over against another. Each alternative represents a potentially responsible choice for scholarship. Each has advantages and disadvantages, but in theoretical and methodological discourse, it is often the set of problems one is willing to live with that finally determines the stance. Students need to be exposed to exemplars of these wider universes of choice and to the consequences entailed by their acceptance—whether the examples be found within or without the area code assigned to religious studies.

Time prevents more than a telegraphic citation of some of these issues. Each deserves long and careful study. To allude to just two: one of the issues that has exercised the American Academy of Religion of late concerns the issues of privilege with respect to the interpretative enterprise. Is the interpreter privileged with respect to the native or to that which is being interpreted? Is the native, or the indigenous exegetical tradition, privileged with respect to the interpreter? Such issues are at least as old as Kant,[17] and while they have been raised recently within religious studies, they are also being hotly debated in most of the fields within the human sciences—especially within literary studies and anthropology.[18] Is the controlling metaphor for relating and understanding an "other" that of photograph, text, or dialogue? These questions are generic to the human sciences and encourage wide, corporate discussion and debate among our varied conversation partners.

Quite similar is that issue which is signaled by the shorthand term, "reductionism" over which much ink has been spilled. On examination this turns out to be a pseudo-issue. It is not that there are reductive disciplines as opposed to nonreductive ones ("We're O.K....but take care, the next tribe over is cannibalistic"), even supposing that we could agree on an adequate definition of "reductionism." A far broader issue appears to be at stake. For example, in *Ideology and Utopia,* Karl Mannheim distinguishes between "right wing" and "left wing" methodologies of the human sciences. The "right wing," he argues,

> tend to use morphological categories which do not break up the concrete totality of the data of experience, but seek rather to preserve it in all its uniqueness. As opposed to this morphological approach [characteristic of the "right"], the analytical approach characteristic of the parties of the left, broke down every concrete totality in order to arrive at smaller, more general units which might then be recombined (in thought).[19]

Redescribing the matter in this fashion, in terms of conservative and radical, eliminates the usual discourse in which the parties of the "right" tend to be all too readily identified with the nonreductive, and smokes out the other sorts of ideological assumptions involved in this seemingly intuitively correct approach: no more good guys and bad guys. Parties of the "left" and "right," "lumpers" and "splitters," "hedgehogs" and "foxes," the "hermeneutics of recovery" and the "hermeneutics of suspicion"—these are coeval and coequal possibilities which can be entertained responsibly by scholars within each of the human sciences. I do not mean to suggest the absence of difference, only to insist that real intellectual differences may well need to be reconfigured in other than traditional disciplinary modes (*scilicet,* departments) around issues basic to all of the human sciences.[20]

This leads to my final point. There is a growing recognition that there may no longer be a set of clear and interesting distinctions between the humanities (broadly conceived) and the social sciences (equally broadly understood). It is a view which, rhetorically, is best expressed in Geertz's classic 1980 essay, "Blurred Genres," in which the interpretive turn ascendent in both the humanities and the social sciences

> is a phenomenon general enough and distinctive enough to suggest that what we are seeing is not just another redrawing of the cultural map—the moving of a few disputed borders...but an alternation of the principles of mapping. Something is happening to the way in which we think about the way we think...[it is] a culture shift... [a] refiguration of social thought....It is not an interdisciplinary brotherhood that is needed, nor even less highbrow eclecticisim. It is recognition on all sides that the lines grouping scholars together into intellectual communities, or (what is the same thing) sorting them out into different ones, are these days running at some highly eccentric angles.[21]

It is a view proposed in operational terms by the University of Chicago's 1982 "Report of the Commission on Graduate Education" (on which I served), which argued:

> There seems to be a growing sense among humanists and social scientists that the customary disciplinary divisions are collapsing. New forms of intellectual discourse are appearing that are erasing the conventional lines of demarcation between the humanities and the social sciences, on the one hand, while realigning their component disciplines on the other....We may well be experiencing a sea-change in the human sciences, a transformation of intellectual boundaries and a reorientation of intellectual interests comparable to that which created the principle disciplines as we know them scarcely a century ago.[22]

In its early discussions, members of the commission argued for removing Ph.D. granting powers from individual departments in the humanities and social sciences and vesting them in an Institute for the Human Sciences with the notion that students would do some significant fraction of their work in courses within the institute and would constitute their dissertation committees from its members. In its published report, the commission kept the intellectual notion but bowed to political realism. It recommended the establishment of an institute for research in the human sciences (or, that failing, two institutes, one in the humanities, one in the social sciences) as the locus of "research and writing leading to the dissertation," but now under departmental supervision. Furthermore, a series of standing seminars and workshops, with faculty and graduate student membership, were to be located in these institutes "to investigate fundamental problems...without limitation by departmental or divisional boundaries."[23] (These latter have been established under an administrative committee without adopting the bulk of the commission's recommendations.) Furthermore, the commission recommended the creation of a parallel series of "wide" Ph.D. programs "in the humanities [or the social sciences] or possibly in the humanities *and* social sciences, which would educate graduate students, or some of them, more liberally and less narrowly than we have done so far."[24]

From such a point of view, the second pedagogical and programmatic question: "To what extent should graduate training in religious studies be intradepartmental and to what extent interdepartmental?" becomes moot. For educational purposes (not to speak of intellectual ends), departments ought to be considered invisible.

To pick up an analogy from the conference document, our present, time-bound topography of fields of study may be seen, at best, as dialects within a far broader language system which has priority of claim upon both the students' and the scholars' attention. That old Latin tag from Terence, revived with such force in those Renaissance and Enlightenment academies that gave rise to the study of religion—"Nothing human is foreign to me"—might now be revised: "Nothing in the human sciences is foreign to me."

Notes

Soundings 61, no. 2/3 (Summer/Fall 1988): 231–44. © by the Society for Values in Higher Education and the University of Tennessee, Knoxville, 1988. Reprinted by permission.

1. All references to "the conference document" are to Gerald James Larson, "The Working Paper: Revising Graduate Education," appendix to *Soundings* 61, no. 2/3 (Summer/Fall 1988): 415–420.

2. Quoted in Eric J. Sharpe, *Comparative Religion: A History* (London: Duckworth Press, 1975), 122. [For Smith's account of this disciplinary history, see in this

volume "Religious Studies: Whither (Wither) and Why?" 64–72 passim; also Smith, "A Twice-told Tale: The History of the History of Religions' History," in *Relating Religion: Essays in the Study of Religion* (Chicago: University of Chicago Press, 2004), 362–374.—Ed.]

3. Emphases original. It would be a worthwhile project to collect legal definitions of "religion." "Religion" was a juridical term long before it became an academic one.

4. Compare these two paragraphs with "Religious Studies: Whither (Wither) and Why," 69.—Ed.

5. Herbert J. Fingarette, *The Self in Transformation* (New York: Harper & Row, 1963), 237.

6. Jonathan Z. Smith, *Imagining Religion* (Chicago: University of Chicago Press, 1982), xi [slightly revised].

7. See R. G. A. Dolby, "Classification of the Sciences: The Nineteenth Century Tradition," in *Classifications in Their Social Context*, ed. Roy F. Ellen and David Reason (London: Academic Press, 1979), 167–193.

8. See, for example, the following statement by Harold Perkin, Director of the Center for Social History, University of Lancaster: "History is the maverick among disciplines, the misfit, the bull in the china shop. Since everything has a history and history, potentially at least, deals with everything that has ever happened in human society, the historian is a kind of licensed rustler who wanders at will across his scholarly neighbors' fields, poaching their stock and purloining their crops and breaking down their hedges. In a very real sense it is not a discipline at all.... The historian can never say, like the physicist or the economist or the theologian, 'That is not my subject'... it may best be described as a concern with change and stability." Harold Perkin, "The Historical Perspective," in *Perspectives on Higher Education: Eight Disciplinary and Comparative Views*, ed. Burton R. Clark (Berkeley: University of California Press, 1984), 17–18.

9. See the more extended discussion of Toulmin and disciplinary self-definition in "To Double Business Bound," 144–47.—Ed.

10. Stephen Toulmin, *Human Understanding*, vol. 1, *The Collective Use and Evolution of Concepts* (Princeton, NJ: Princeton University Press, 1972), 380–381.

11. Thomas S. Kuhn, *The Structure of Scientific Revolutions*, 2nd ed. (Chicago: University of Chicago Press, 1970), 15–17.

12. Smith, *Imagining Religion*, xi–xii [slightly revised].

13. "Here and Now: Prospects for Graduate Education," 40 (slightly revised).

14. Charles Hartshorne and William L. Reese, *Philosophers Speak of God* (Chicago: University of Chicago Press, 1963), 1–25. See the other literature cited in Hans H. Penner, "Bedeutung und Probleme der religiösen Symbolik bei Tillich und Eliade," *Antaios* 9 (1967): 127–143.

15. I toy here with Melford E. Spiro, "Religion: Problems of Definition and Explanation," in *Anthropological Approaches to the Study of Religion*, ed. Michael Banton (London: Tavistock Publications, 1966), 96.

16. Alfred Rupp, *Phänomenon und Geschichte: Prolegomena zur Methodologie der Religionsgeschichte* (Saarbrücken: Homo et Religio, 1978) and the review by Kurt Rudolph, *Numen*, 27 (1980): 180–185.

17. Immanuel Kant, *Critique of Pure Reason,* trans. Norman K. Smith (London: Macmillan, 1956), 310 (B 370). See further the discussion of Hans-Georg Gadamer, *Truth and Method*, translation edited by Garrett Barden and John Cumming (New York: Seabury Press, 1975), 170–171 for a brief history of the notion.

18. See among others, George E. Marcus and Michael M. J. Fischer, *Anthropology as Cultural Critique: An Experimental Moment in the Human Sciences* (Chicago: University of Chicago Press, 1986).

19. Karl Mannheim, *Ideology and Utopia* (New York: Harcourt Brace, 1936), 274.

20. On the intellectual incoherence and political threat of departments, and related matters, see also "Connections," 55–56; "Religious Studies: Whither (Wither) and Why?" 69 passim; "Re-Forming the Undergraduate Curriculum," 107–08; and "Why the College Major?" 113–14.—Ed.

21. Clifford Geertz, "Blurred Genres," reprinted in Geertz, *Local Knowledge* (New York: Basic Books, 1983), 19–35. I have taken the passages quoted from pages 20, 19, 23–24.

22. "Report of the Commission on Graduate Education," *University of Chicago Record* 16, no. 2 (1982): 169.

23. "Report," 171–172.

24. "Report," 159.

PART II

The Academic Profession

9

Re-forming the Undergraduate Curriculum: A Retrospective

TO INVITE AN historian, especially one concerned largely with archaic and somewhat arcane matters such as the history of culture or the history of religion, to be "retrospective," "to situate the contemporary discussion of the structure of the undergraduate curriculum" was quite possibly rash. It is true I have spent much time engaged in that discussion, as a college dean, as a member of the Association of American Colleges Select Committee on the Baccalaureate Degree (whose published report, *Integrity in the College Curriculum*, was one year old last week) and as a sometimes writer and speaker on educational matters.[1] But...contemporaneity be damned. What historical fire dog would not respond to a bell summoning "historical context"? Having said this, I must warn you at the outset that I am not an historian of education. I know little more than I believe every faculty member ought to know as a part of his or her professional responsibility. Moreover, I will narrate and reflect on part of that history, not in order to edify, but rather to make a point.

While I have resisted the temptation to begin with the first educational documents in Western civilization—those Sumerian school texts from c. 2500 B.C. published by Samuel Noah Kramer in the *Journal of the American Oriental Society* in 1949[2]—I do want to remind you, at the outset, that there is nothing so very new about the sorts of issues that I presume led to the formation of this Academic Forum and to this meeting. In 1909, an 1899 graduate of the University of California complained about the education he had received in this manner: "All these studies were simply separate tasks that bore no definite intrinsic relation to each other...The right studies were there; what was lacking was the conscious organization of them for the student."[3]

This issue of "conscious organization," and the question of who should provide the organization—the faculty for the student, the student out of the faculty's offerings—might provide nodes around which to gather our discussion.

In truth, in so framing matters in an attempt to be affable at the outset, I have been overly generous. The question just raised is no question at all. By charter, by statute, by any notion of faculty responsibility, not to speak of by student fee, it is the faculty *alone* who is charged with providing organization. To do otherwise is to violate what my colleagues at Chicago have taken to calling Smith's iron law: *A student may not be asked to integrate what the faculty will not.*

The issue of organization, a matter which is prior in every sense of the word, will not be so easily dismissed by rhetoric, although it is to the rhetorical tradition that I would turn to gain a taxonomy of possible answers to the issue of organization. Anyone who has read through the major studies of the early conceptions of the liberal arts curriculum— L. J. Paetow, *The Arts Course at Medieval Universities*; P. Abelson, *The Seven Liberal Arts*[4]—will have been struck by a sharp dichotomy between the classical and medieval understanding of the liberal arts on the one hand, and the Renaissance understanding on the other. For the former, the liberal arts were perceived as skills, capacities, ways of doing; for the latter, they were understood to be fields, areas, contents, subject matters. These two understandings, or, more commonly, a combination or muddle of the two, will determine the vast majority of curricular organizations in American institutions of higher learning. However, we need to take a more leisurely route to this conclusion and its implications.

As I persist in teaching my students, within the wordy world of human sciences, the proper way to begin an argument is by an act of definition.[5] It is only then that there is something on the table which you and I might agree to take as a datum for purposes of the argument. So, we need to begin by getting liberal education on the table. It is a task that is more difficult than one might have anticipated. Not because of its gravity, but because it is so damned airy-fairy. Even the enterprise of lexical definition, that most humdrum of all definitory endeavors, proves problematic. This is not because we don't know in some fashion or other what we mean—we can all point to ourselves—but because the word itself has been constantly redefined, preserving, palimpsest-like, all of its previous connotations, unadjusted and intact.

The question clearly focuses on the adjective, "liberal." It suggests that there is a species, "liberal," of the genus, "education," and that there are other sorts of education which, by way of contrast, were meant to be excluded. A good, historical lexicon clarifies the matter. The initial distinction was between the liberal arts and the "servile arts," the former, according to the *Oxford English Dictionary*, being those "worthy of a freeman, pertaining to persons of superior social status, i.e., a gentleman." The *OED* goes on to illustrate the connotation of the word, "liberal," in liberal arts or liberal education with the following quotation from 1801: "Two centuries back, horse racing was conceived as a liberal pastime, practiced for pleasure not for profit."

The implications are clear, even if they are, today, socially unacceptable. Liberal education was designed to benefit a fairly homogenous social class, with at least a modicum of wealth and a shared culture and worldview, which looked forward, above all, to having considerable free time. Colleges were designed to impart a certain savoir-faire, a broad civil, cultural, and civic veneer to a group of largely middle- and upper-class students (predominantly male) for most of whom positions were waiting and leisure assured. These colleges were designed to lay the foundations for the fruitful enjoyment of the *nonworking* portions of their students' lives, by introducing them to an appreciation for, and conventions of discourse about, the arts, and to a broad range of intellectual and historical generalizations which would serve to make them informed, urbane laypersons and citizens. Liberal learning, in this first definition, was the acquisition of the civilized art of gossip.

In such a curriculum, there could be no question as to what constituted the knowledge most worth having, for there was no dissonance. Knowledge was, above all, knowledge about oneself (they called it "character" in those days) and those precedents for oneself that could be found in the past (they called those the "classics"). It is the sort of world proudly exemplified in the writings of one of the greatest of modern-day snobs, hence one of the recent incarnations of the old ideal of liberal education, the late art historian, Bernard Berenson, when he wrote: "Significant events are those which have contributed to making us what we are to-day. Art history must avoid what has not contributed to the mainstream, no matter how interesting, how magnificent in itself."[6]

Berenson goes on to state clearly the consequences of such a position. Art history ought to ignore all the arts of Asia, Africa, and the Americas, as it should ignore most German, Spanish, and Dutch art, as well as Italian art after the eighteenth century. For, he writes, none of these are "of universal appeal to cultivated Europeans." From such a vantage point, education was never seen as a process of confrontation, but rather, always, of confirmation.

There was, as well, a second implication to the original distinction between the "liberal" and the "servile," and that led to purging the space of liberal education from anything that smacked of the "trades." The ideology of the campus was plain: if the professors (hopefully) were to be revered, the professions, everything that related to the work-a-day nine-to-five world, were to be reviled. They represented, in both word and deed, a contagious source of impurity within the sanctum.

This first view of liberal education has been taken by many to have achieved classic formulation in the curricula of the great fourteenth-century French universities where the entire four years were devoted to studying the logical, physical, and ethical treatises of Aristotle. However, lest you think this is arcane irrelevance, please recall that the 1830–31 catalog of Harvard (ironically reproduced as the frontispiece in E. K. Rand's *Founders of the Middle Ages*[7]) shows that the first two years of college study were, then, largely devoted to classes conducted by the recitation method in Livy, Homer, the Greek New Testament, Horace, Hesiod, Tacitus, Cicero, and Pliny. While we associate President Charles Eliot with the introduction of the elective system at Harvard (which did much to unravel this classical consensus), perhaps his greatest revolution, proposed in his inaugural address of 1869, was the introduction of English literature into the curriculum—an innovation first carried out at Lafayette College, between 1857–60, where Francis March taught Milton and Shakespeare "as if they were classics."

As Frederick Rudolph has argued in his magisterial work *Curriculum: A History of the Undergraduate Course of Study Since 1636*, a book which, alongside Arthur Levine's *Handbook on the Undergraduate Curriculum*, should be required reading for all faculty members, the period following the Civil War was one of the great watersheds of American curricular experimentation.[8] America became newly conscious of itself as a single nation, its renewed sense of the vastness of the continent, the beginning of the process of breaking down, to some degree, caste and class— all these suggested the need for an enlarged view of knowledge which resulted in the importation of the German model of the university; the creation of a new mode of academic polity, the department; the formation of graduate programs; stronger emphasis on the sciences; and the introduction of the elective. In short, all of the innovations we associate with the great antebellum generation of university presidents: Ezra Cornell, Andrew White, Daniel Gilman, and Charles Eliot. On the other hand, the long-standing American commitment to a more practical dimension to education (already present in Ben Franklin's *Proposals Relating to the Education of Youth in Pennsylvania* [1749]) became intensified after the Civil War, and, coupled with the pressure to expand the base of those who were college educated (from the 1.7 percent of the college-age population in 1870) led to the rapid development of the Land Grant colleges during the same period and the introduction, in the 1890s, of professional option programs at many of the private universities' colleges.

In terms of the early history of the word, the innovations rendered the original connotations of "liberal education" problematic, or, at least, inconvenient. Accordingly, the understanding of the adjective, "liberal," was radically shifted from something aristocratic to something rather more democratic. "Liberal" in liberal education, we will now be told (using a false etymology), means liberating, a setting free. As this brings us to familiar territory, to the sort of rhetoric which is commonplace in contemporary colleges, I can be briefer in my description.

In this second understanding of "liberal," the majority of the older elements persist with a somewhat different flavor: the language of individual development, of character; a reading list of so-called classic texts which are thought to display, almost always anachronistically, the emergence of ideals such as freedom, democracy, self, and individualism. At the same time, the curriculum expressed liberation by introducing electivity, the student's inalienable right to make an individual (and usually uninformed) choice.

Added were two notions of somewhat different pedigree which resulted, in four-year colleges, in the introduction of the major.[9] The one was the notion of liberating the mind from dogma or habit, sometimes expressed through the slogan of "critical inquiry," more usually through celebrations of the Weberian research ideal. The other was a shift from the aristocratic notion of the leisure-time dilettante to the acceptance of the middle-class work ethic of professionalism (as chronicled in B. J. Bledstein's study, *The Culture of Professionalism*[10]); "Arbeit ist Freiheit." Most liberal arts colleges became, despite their earlier and still lingering rhetoric, preprofessional endeavors of unprecedented proportions as they eventually came to see one of their chief functions to be the preparation of their students for the vocation of being postbaccalaureate students, above all, for entrance (despite the actual plans of the vast majority of their students) into the academic profession. Collegiate education was shamelessly transformed into *under*graduate education—a phenomenon that reached fantastic heights in the late sixties.

The system that emerged from this history was the present uneasy compromise between two fundamentally incompatible views. Colleges' rhetoric about what is liberal in what they do reflects finishing school notions of liberal learning characteristic of the first phase. Colleges' rhetoric of concentration and depth largely reflects notions associated with the second phase. What one academic spokesman at Brown expressed as a pious hope in 1908, that "all the stronger institutions" might mingle "in due proportion...the best from the old English-American college with the best from the modern German university" had been realized.[11] The result seemed to many, not a golden mean but a leaden muddle.

Reactions were varied and fragments or entire pieces of these reforms still operate on many college campuses, alongside the conflicting, generative models they were designed to modify or replace, thus exacerbating rather than ameliorating the confusion. To review this more familiar ground somewhat rapidly:

(1) There was renewed interest in the major/minor (first introduced at Johns Hopkins in 1878) joined with the distribution requirement developed at Harvard in 1909. This combination remains, to this day, the most common mode of introducing an aura of coherence to the curriculum. However, such arrangements only require the repackaging of already existing courses and components so as to give a facade of organization while preserving student electivity.

(2) The widespread experimentation with honors programs in the period immediately preceding World War I emphasized individuality. To quote one of the early advocates, Swarthmore's president, "it [the honors program] is based on the theory that each person is unique, that each deserves to have his own powers developed to the fullest possible extent."[12] Coherence, in such programs, was often more personal, whether reflecting mentor or student, and the format followed suit: small classes, seminar, close contact between students and faculty, emphasis on individual research project often with an interdisciplinary (or idiosyncratic) cast. Honors programs, translated into organizational schema and curricula, are writ large in many of the experimental colleges of the past two decades. In these, what was designed as a distinctive alternative for a subset within a larger college or university, has, at

institutions such as Hampshire and New College (Florida), become the norm.

(3) The development of largely nonfaculty and administrative networks (beginning in the 1890s and commonplace by 1920) for individually guiding the student through the maze of curricular choices voted by the faculty—orientation programs, the new profession of academic advising, introductory courses on how to learn in college—reinforce the old saw: faculty design curricula, students take programs.

These, and other innovations, added to the antebellum redefinition of undergraduate education, provoked a perhaps inevitable conservative backlash. Even figures such as Andrew White came to lament: "We have too much lost sight of certain valuable old things, the things...which used to be summed up under the word *culture*."[13]

Intensified by World War I and by the trauma of the American Depression, "general education" became a new rallying cry. The introduction of the required Western Civilization course at Columbia, destined to become the single most popular required course at colleges across the country,[14] together with a course on the classics of Western literature and thought, and the more ambitious attempts at general education via the "Great Books" at Chicago, associated with Robert M. Hutchins, continued to this day at St. John's, and recently atavistically celebrated by William J. Bennett in his report *To Reclaim a Legacy*,[15] were the most visible and enduring results.

The remarks on the "Great Books" curricula delivered by Albert William Levi in 1968 deserve quotation:

It is instructive to compare the critical reaction to this proposal then and now. The first responses reflected dismay at the number and heterogeneity of the works included. How in a mere four-year period could one possibly do justice to 100 books as rich and demanding as Plato's Republic...Gibbon's *Decline and Fall of the Roman Empire*...[Levi names a dozen or so titles]...Above all, where would one find those polymaths—learned in the entire spectrum of the arts and sciences—who could instruct with equal competence whether the materials were Euclidean geometry, ancient Greek history, medieval epic, Renaissance physics, baroque drama, the nineteenth century novel, or contemporary psychoanalytical theory? The trouble with this cultural baggage was that it was too heavy a load to carry, and those who adopted the program found it necessary to slowly cut...excise...until the weight grew more manageable. But at this point the program could more justly have been called not the "great books" but the "great pamphlets" of the western world; something like the *Summa Theologica* of St. Thomas Aquinas cut to fit the requirements of *The Readers Digest*! Today, thirty years later, the tide of criticism has turned—in fact, it has almost completely reversed itself. The trouble lies not in the weight but in the lightness, in the provincialism of the phrase "western culture" in a world where Katanga is more important than Canterbury, Laos than Los Angeles, Vietnam than Vienna. The Hutchins-Adler list, we now see, contains not too many items, but too few. Culture has outrun the European heartland to encompass the world.[16]

Regardless of these criticisms (and others I would make which would be even sharper[17]), there is an important lesson to be learned from the Columbia/Chicago experiment in general education. Coherence and organization will not emerge from merely rearranging already existing courses by a process that resembles Lévi-Strauss's "bricolage"; it will only be achieved by *courses specifically designed to fulfill widely agreed upon educational purposes.*

Please pause and reflect for a moment on the history I've so rapidly reviewed. Note that for all of this diversity, each of the educational programs I have thus far described has one characteristic in common: in some form or other, they subscribe to the Renaissance understanding of the liberal arts. That is to say, in one way or another, they each view education as essentially concerned with fields, areas, contents, subject matters. This is *not* the direction in which much contemporary curricular discussion seems to be heading.

In the past two and a half years, we have been presented with a series of dire reports on the state of American education.[18] The majority (Thank God!) have focused on secondary education, towards which those of us in higher education continue to act as if we have no responsibility, although we train all of its teachers and administrators. Some half dozen have concentrated on collegiate education. Only one has examined the holy of holies—graduate education. I will not rehearse their jeremiads, the popular press has done a fulsome job of that. Rather I want to direct your attention to one of the commonalities that might be discerned. Expressed in different ways in the College Board report, the report of the Association of

State Colleges and Universities, the report of the Association of American Colleges, and others, there is a *shift from a language of topics and subjects to a language of skills and capacities.* If this is a forecast of the future shape of curricular discussions, as I believe it is, then it marks a return to the classical and medieval understandings of the liberal arts as, preeminently, ways of doing.

Let me indicate, briefly, some of the sorts of possibilities that have already emerged from this shift with respect to organization. In so doing, I leave out other important implications, the most significant of which suggests the relaxation (perhaps even the elimination) of the line between the liberal arts programs and programs of preprofessional and professional education—a line which was an essential article of faith for the old definition of liberal learning which persists in much collegiate curricular rhetoric until today.

(1) The most traditional is the widely publicized Harvard core. While remaining essentially subject oriented, and largely consisting of already existing courses newly baptized and arranged according to a modified distribution pattern, it does have one suggestive feature: the requirement that each core course be tested by a faculty committee for its self-consciously generalizing nature, i.e., the degree to which it can articulate a transcendence of its subject matter to reveal characteristic modes of thought. A somewhat similar rationale lies behind the newer incarnations of Chicago's forty-five-year-old "core." As expressed in slogan form: "Not what is thought, but how it is thought." The major practical difference is that Chicago's courses were initially designed and are being continuously reworked by groups of faculty with this end in view.

(2) A number of small colleges (e.g., Haverford) have made the interesting experiment of constructing what Benjamin Bloom would call a taxonomy of educational objectives and requiring each student to experience each of them.[19] Using numerical codes, they label each of their courses, identifying which one or more of these objectives each course fulfills regardless of subject matter. In other words, they have superimposed a general map of skills and capacities on a traditional catalog arranged by subject matter.

(3) Somewhat more radically, the recent Association of American Colleges report, *Integrity in the College Curriculum*, proposes a list of nine "experiences" every baccalaureate candidate should have had in his or her four-year course of study. "Some of them," the report

states, "might be thought of as skills, others as ways of growing and understanding." In no case, the report insists, are these experiences to be associated with particular courses or programs. The report is not advocating "solving the curricular problems of higher education by simply strengthening distribution requirements or adding multi-disciplinary general education courses. We believe that either one of these old solutions is more likely to perpetuate rather than to remedy the conditions that brought our committee into existence."[20] Rather, these experiences should "find outlets and encouragement across the curriculum," and their fulfillment should be tested for by instruments of each institution's design.

(4) Finally, and most formalistically of all, one notes the recent mandate of the California legislature that at least one course in "critical thinking" be required of every baccalaureate candidate. While the impulse is to be honored, one can only shudder at its formulation. The law requires a course which trains in the "defensive abilities" of critical thinking such as the abilities to separate fact from judgment, belief from knowledge—a sort of black-belt theory of education about which I need say no more except that I expect similar requirements to become common.

As promising as I believe this shift from topics to capacities to be, I doubt it will get us very far. For the issues we confront are not solely intellectual ones, but also, or above all, *political* ones. *The precondition for serious curricular discourse is the acceptance by the faculty as a whole of responsibility for the totality of the curriculum; the prerequisite for serious curricular action is the acceptance of the principle of the utter accountability of each part to the whole.*

Let me illustrate this at a sanitary distance so as not to abuse my role as guest by examining with you in some detail the single most thoughtful institutional curricular report that I know of, Harvard's so-called Red Book of 1945, *General Education in a Free Society*.[21] Although the report was rejected by the Harvard faculty, it stands, even today, as the remembered or unacknowledged gospel behind most college curricula. Its rhetoric remains the characteristic rhetoric of some of our most thoughtful and devoted college faculty.

After an introductory chapter which reveals, from our present vantage point, its wartime and immediately postwar setting, the report stakes out its primary curricular claims in chapter 2, "Theory of General Education." It begins with a series of dialectical statements (at least that's what a theologian would call them; others, with less Christian charity, might term them confused or contradictory), a set of both/and propositions which fail to achieve the level of theory. To wit, education "must uphold at the same time tradition and experiment" (51), general education must "combine fixity of aim with diversity of application" (57), "capable at once of taking on many different forms and yet of representing in all its forms the common knowledge and common values on which a free society depends" (58).

Having thus outdone Parmenides, the report turns, in the third and fourth sections of its "Theory," to what it terms "the actual outcomes of general education," asking two questions which it perceives to be intrinsically interrelated. "What characteristics (traits of mind and character) are necessary for anything like a full and responsible life in our society?"—the aim of liberal education. And, "By what elements of knowledge are such traits nourished?" The report insists that "these two questions are images of each other" (58), and, as if to reinforce this mirror-like quality, proceeds to reverse the topics, treating in section 3, "Areas of Knowledge," and in section 4, "Traits of Mind."

In its section, "Areas of Knowledge," the report proposes a classification of the "traditional" three areas of learning: the natural sciences, social studies, and the humanities. It rejects as inadequate the "obvious even trite" division by subject matter on two grounds. "Subject matters do not lend themselves to such easy distinctions"; their example is psychology, but "a more serious flaw in this classification is that it conceives of education as the act of getting acquainted with something...as the acquiring of information." It proposes, instead, to divide the areas of learning "in terms of methods of knowledge" (59).

The natural sciences, it is claimed, "describe, analyze, and explain"; the humanities "appraise, judge and criticize" (59). The former ask questions as to "truth" and "reality"; the latter, questions of "value" (60ff). This logical classification by division is then perturbed and made messy. Social studies "combine the methods of the natural sciences and the humanities," they "use both explanation and evaluation" (61). So the distinctions turn out to be no distinctions at all. In the words of the report, they are "rough and inexact; the total area of learning is more like a spectrum along which the diverse modes of thought are combined in various degrees, approximating to purity only at the extreme ends" (63).

Harvard giveth, and Harvard taketh away. Praised be the name of Harvard! Why the taking away? Some wag (or Yalie) might suggest that the consequences of their position might have led to the conclusion that social studies ought to make up the sole content of general education because it provides the golden mean—"it combines the methods of the natural sciences and the humanities." Or, reversing the logic, since social studies is a mixture of what is found "approximating to purity" elsewhere, it might be altogether excluded from general education. However, a closer reading of the text will dismiss such flip hypotheses. In fact, what caused the perturbation was that the worthy Dons forgot their subject matter. They fulfilled the absent-minded stereotype of their profession.

You will recall that they began their enterprise by proposing to classify three "areas of knowledge." However, in their discussion, they rapidly wandered off into debates about the placement of psychology, history, philosophy, and mathematical economics. That is to say, in Linnaean terms, they began with discourse about phyla and rapidly switched to gossip about species, varieties, and hybrids. The perturbation was brought about by substituting the cartography of departments for the taxonomy of areas of knowledge. It was an instinctive (and prophetic) retreat to more familiar and comfortable turf.

This is not all. The taxonomy was also blurred by design. It was offered only to be set aside. The goal of liberal learning (despite what we might have thought on the basis of their original claims) does not turn out to be, after all, the appreciation of the informing power and attendant economy of the several methods and areas of knowledge, but rather their relativization. As the last sentence of this section reads: "To the extent that the student becomes aware of the methods he is using, and critically conscious of his presuppositions, he learns to transcend his specialty and generates a liberal outlook in himself" (64).

Beyond the somewhat awkward and gnostic picture of the student's self-conversion and self-redemption—especially at Harvard's tuition rates—this is an extraordinary claim. The purpose of the study of the "methods of knowledge" is to become nonmethodical, that is to say, in the report's phrase, "liberal." (I may add, as an aside, that it is far from easy to distinguish this sense of being "liberal" from a posture of cynicism.)

Given the quixotic conclusion to the section devoted to "Methods of Knowledge," that the purpose of the study of methods is to become non-methodical, we turn to the next section of the report, "Traits of Mind" with justifiable trepidation. Could its conclusion be that a student after four years ought to become mindless? But... not to worry. The first paragraph, at least, allays anxiety after beginning in an unpromising way. "Education is not a process of stuffing the mind with facts," for the student "soon forgets not only many facts but even [*sic*] some general ideas and principles." (A claim no doubt adequately substantiated by Harvard's well-known series of longitudinal surveys.) Rather, the purpose of education is "the cultivation of certain aptitudes and attitudes in the mind of the young," a set of "characteristics" of mind. So strongly does the report feel the force of this claim that it goes on to draw its prescriptive consequences. These "characteristics prescribe how general education ought to be carried out and which abilities should be sought above all others in every part of it" (64). A principle of corporate accountability is here being enunciated. If meant, it should be applauded.

What, then, are these "characteristics" which serve as both the goal of the educational enterprise and the criteria by which its several parts might be judged? No surprise; they are the abilities "to think effectively, to communicate thought, to make relevant judgments, to discriminate among values" (65). While there is a typical cognitive bias to these "characteristics," they are not at all foreign to the majority of us or to the stated goals of the institutions we serve. They are, in fact, our stock-in-trade. There are few of us that would quarrel with this list or with the report's subsequent characterizations of effective thinking, communication, judgment, and values. But, such agreement begs the difficult question. What is the relationship between the two foundational elements in the report's theory of education: forms of knowledge and qualities of mind? These were held to be mirror images of each other. How is this reciprocity to be institutionalized in the curriculum and its courses?

The plain fact is that the report is confused—as are we—on just this point. It offers five quite different sorts of answers to this question which represent a map of traditional curricular strategies and traditional curricular disarray.

(1) It affirms a correlation. "The three phases of effective thinking, logical, relational and imaginative, correspond roughly to the three divisions of learning, the natural sciences, the social studies and the humanities, respectively" (67). In other words, a course on science is offered to display and develop the capacity for logical thinking; that in social studies, for relational thinking; that in humanities, for imaginative thinking.

(2) It suggests a focus on "characteristics" regardless of course subject. "Every course, whether general or special, may be expected to contribute something to all of these abilities" (74); "general education must...be conceived less as a specific set of books to be read or courses

to be given, than as a concern for certain goals of knowledge and outlook and an insistence that these goals be sought after by as many means as intently as are those of specialism" (80). Note that these two proposals are, at the very least, in tension with each other. The one suggests that there are certain "abilities" that correspond to the distinctive "methods" of the several "areas of knowledge." The other insists that any and every area of knowledge "may be expected to contribute something to all of these abilities" (74). The example offered for this latter is revealing, for it shows that, once again, it is not, in fact, areas of knowledge that are being thought of, as the report defined them, but rather departments.[22] History, the report argues, should be as concerned as English with a student's ability to express himself; history should be as concerned as mathematics for a student's ability to think logically (74). As the report turned its attention to more concrete curricular proposals, this initial tension became enlarged. It proposes six courses in general education, "of the six, at least one shall be [a required course] in the humanities, one in the social sciences and one in the sciences" (196).

(3) These courses "should achieve the aims of general education" (197), that is to say, fulfill the particular contribution to the development of the "qualities of mind" exhibited by each of the three "forms of knowledge."

However, (4) in its statement of purpose, this goal appears to have been abandoned. Rather than "qualities of mind" and "distinctive methods," it is content and socialization that is to govern these courses. They "would be expected to furnish the common core, the body of learning and ideas which would be a common experience of all Harvard students" (196). In the language I used earlier, they would enhance gossip rather than intellectual discourse.

(5) This confusion becomes even more apparent in the specific descriptions of the required courses—the report's fifth set of recommendations. All pretense of concern for "logical, relational and imaginative modes of thought," for "communication," and "judgment," and "values" has been dropped. What is proposed is a course on "Great Texts of Western Literature" (205), a course on "Western Thought and Institutions" (213) [that is to say, the Columbia schema] and, the giveaway, in the case of the natural sciences, "it is proposed that there be established alternative courses to meet the needs of those students who come to college with marked divergences in their preparations and plans for special study, as well as with disparities in their competence

in dealing with mathematical and scientific material" (196). So much for the notion of a required course on the "logical" aspects of "effective thinking"!

I have spent time on this classic text of curricular reform, not in order to beat a dead horse, but to confront an exceedingly live one. For in highly articulate form, this report has set forth the common rationale behind the flaccid curricular schema of almost all of our present day institutions of higher learning—whether their goals be addressed through cores, distribution requirements, or survey courses. The report exhibits with uncommon clarity the deep tensions underlying such organizations. For the Harvard report was not merely an attempt at achieving an intellectual and educational charter, it was, as well, a proposal for a political deal.

Note what the report discussed and what it omitted. Beyond some gentlemanly tut-tuttings about "specialism," it left wholly unexamined the concentration or major. It conceded, in advance, the major's self-proclaimed rationale without scrutiny. It asked no questions concerning the adequacy of departmental organizations of knowledge—indeed its arguments presumed them in place. Instead, it developed a woefully abstract scheme of the divisions of knowledge and an equally generalized set of mental qualities that conformed to this division. This conscious abstraction was a political act of the first magnitude, for, having done so, having projected a curricular space that belonged in principle to everyone but in fact belonged to no one—indeed, it is doubtful that it would be in anyone's interest to inhabit it—it then proceeded to give away the store: on the one hand, to old genteel ideas of common literacy which have more to do with a nostalgia for civility than with the development of "mental qualities"; on the other hand, to departmental claims to own or incarnate particular domains of thought. Furthermore, having constructed these modes of thought in so abstract and empty a fashion, it could guarantee their ultimate irrelevance. The final goal of liberal learning, you will recall, was their transcendence.

Translated into political terms, this vague, contradictory, abstract, and implausible definition of general education, in fact, gave all power to what the report terms "specialism." It created the rationale for the trade-off which resulted in our present condition, where, as Fred Rudolph notes, "by 1976, the concentration or major was in charge of the curriculum."[23] By locating all public scrutiny, all corporate responsibility on the side of the vaguely stated and abstract aims of general education, the report, in fact, freed the major and departmental concerns from all responsible testing. It gave aid and comfort to that most pernicious of faculty political claims, that of "departmental autonomy"—a perverse notion, different from, indeed opposed to, the laudatory claim of academic freedom.[24]

Although majors, in most institutions, consume more than half of a student's college career, and far more than half of a faculty member's collegiate teaching effort, the major is held to be largely unaccountable to the wider faculty or institution except in the most ceremonial sense (usually at the moment of its inception). It remains the privileged responsibility of a small group within each institution as well as, to some degree, the larger professional association without. As long as this privilege is unchallenged and in place, it is difficult to imagine corporate faculty discussion of the curriculum as a whole and of the total course of study as experienced by students. But, this is what is required. By and large, the piecemeal reform of curricular organization has failed—it is long past time to reexamine the whole.

If I were to predict the future, a rash prospect for any historian, it would be that the major battles in the next decade with respect to the curriculum will come to be fought out over the question of the self-evidence of the major and its claim on curricular space and effort. This is not so much because of doubts as to its putative intellectual content, although there are those of us who find that not immune from challenge,[25] but rather because of its political hegemony coupled with its fissive, successionist tendencies. It will not be an easy discussion, but it will be a necessary one if the preconditions of acceptance by the faculty for the totality of the curriculum and the utter accountability of each part to the whole are to be met. It is the kind of discussion towards which it is appropriate to ask the questions posed centuries ago by a revered teacher and sage:

If not by us, then, by whom? If not now, then, when?

Notes

James W. Reed, ed., *Re-Forming the Undergraduate Curriculum: Invitation to Dialogue: Inaugural Papers from the Academic Forum* (Rutgers, NJ: Rutgers University Press, 1986), 1–21. Reprinted by permission.

1.   *Integrity in the College Curriculum: A Report to the Academic Community: The Findings and Recommendations of the Project on Redefining the Meaning and Purpose of Baccalaureate Degrees* (Washington, D.C.: Association of American Colleges, 1985).

2. Samuel Noah Kramer, "Schooldays: A Sumerian Composition Relating to the Education of a Scribe," *Journal of the American Oriental Society* 69, no. 4 (Oct.–Dec., 1949): 199–215.

3. Laurence R. Veysey, *The Emergence of the American University* (Chicago: University of Chicago Press, 1965), 114.

4. Louis John Paetow, *The Arts Course at Medieval Universities: With Special Reference to Grammar and Rhetoric* (Urbana-Champaign: University of Illinois Press, 1910); Paul Abelson, *The Seven Liberal Arts: A Study in Medieval Culture* (New York: Teacher's College/Columbia University, 1906).

5. On the pedagogical centrality of definitions, see "Approaching the College Classroom," 6; "The Introductory Course: Less Is Better," 17; and "Scriptures and Histories," 29.—Ed.

6. Bernard Berenson, *Aesthetics and History* (London: Constable, 1950), 257ff.

7. Edward Kennard Rand, *Founders of the Middle Ages* (Cambridge, MA: Harvard University Press, 1928).

8. Frederick Rudolph, *Curriculum: A History of the Undergraduate Course of Study Since 1636* (San Francisco: Jossey-Bass, 1977). Arthur Levine, *Handbook on Undergraduate Curriculum* (San Francisco: Jossey-Bass, 1978).

9. See "Why the College Major?" for an extended discussion.—Ed.

10. Burton J. Bledstein, *The Culture of Professionalism: The Middle Class and the Development of Higher Education in America* (New York: Norton, 1976).

11. Rudolph, *Curriculum*, 204.

12. Rudolph, *Curriculum*, 231.

13. Rudolph, *Curriculum*, 238.

14. See Gilbert Allardyce, "The Rise and Fall of the Western Civilization Course," *American Historical Review* 87, no. 3 (June 1982): 695–725.

15. William J. Bennett, *To Reclaim a Legacy: A Report on the Humanities in Higher Education* (Washington, D.C.: National Endowment for the Humanities, 1984).

16. Albert William Levi, *The Humanities Today* (Bloomington: Indiana University Press, 1970), 69ff.

17. Cf. Smith, "Jonathan Z. Smith on William J. Bennett's 'To Reclaim a Legacy: A Report on the Humanities in Higher Education,'" *American Journal of Education* 93, no. 4 (August 1985): 541–546.

18. Compare this passage with "Towards Imagining New Frontiers," 69.—Ed.

19. Benjamin Samuel Bloom, ed., *Taxonomy of Educational Objectives: The Classification of Educational Goals: By a Committee of College and University Examiners* (New York: D. McKay, 1956–64).

20. *Integrity*, 25.

21. Harvard University, Committee on the Objectives of a General Education in a Free Society, *General Education in a Free Society: Report of the Harvard Committee*, introduction by James Bryant Conant (Cambridge, MA: Harvard University Press, 1945).

22. On the intellectual incoherence and political threat of departments, and related matters, see also "Connections," 55–56; "Religious Studies: Whither (Wither) and Why?" 69 passim; "'Religion' and 'Religious Studies': No Difference At All," 81–82; and "Why the College Major?" 113–114.—Ed.

23. Rudolph, *Curriculum*, 248.

24. See Paul L. Dressel and William H. Faricy, *Return to Responsibility: Constraints on Autonomy in Higher Education*, with Philip M. Marcus and Craig Johnson, foreword by Frederick de W. Bolman (San Francisco: Jossey-Bass, 1972), esp. 15.

25. See "Why the College Major?" 111–119.—Ed.

Why the College Major? Questioning the Great, Unexplained Aspect of Undergraduate Education

What is the function of the major? Most departments
would reply: to provide a basic minimum of speciali-
zation and coverage in a field. But to what end?

—D. BELL

THE COLLEGE MAJOR is the great, unexamined aspect of undergraduate education.[1] Despite its fairly recent introduction into the curriculum, its purpose and design have come to seem all but self-evident. While there are periodic convulsions in institutions of higher learning over general education and its requirements, there has rarely been discussion of the major, save when a particular major is introduced at a given institution and seeks a license. In principle, general education is everybody's business—hence, it all too often becomes nobody's business, especially after the thrill of constructing a new program subsides. But the major is the daily business of a small, quite particular, and often well-organized group of faculty—hence, no one else's business. To be busy about someone else's major is to be a busybody indeed!

Although majors consume more than half of a student's college career, and more than half of a faculty member's teaching effort, the major is held to be largely unaccountable to the wider faculty or institution except in the most ceremonial sense. It remains the privileged responsibility of a small group within the institution as well as, to some degree, the larger profession without. The prime issue confronting the integrity of

the baccalaureate degree is faculty governance, and the assumption of corporate responsibility for the totality of the degree. The failure to assume
such responsibility is most evident in the major.

The history of the major has been recounted (most recently, in
Frederick Rudolph's *Curriculum: A History of the Undergraduate Course of
Study Since 1636*), and its chief claim reiterated at educational conferences,
in college catalogs, and during department meetings. The major, we are
told, was introduced to bring focus and depth to what was perceived as an
unfocused (elective) and overgeneralizing curriculum. But rarely was the
question asked, depth and focus for what? (The answer was assumed to
be self-evident: to begin the training of academics such as ourselves.)

The present four-year liberal arts curriculum is an uneasy compromise growing out of this history. It consists of general requirements (core
or distribution) to introduce breadth, as determined by the faculty; major
requirements to introduce depth as determined by a subset of the faculty;
and electives, which may be used to further either breadth or depth of
study as determined by the student.

In practice, there has been no compromise at all. In the majority of
institutions, as Rudolph has noted, "by 1976, the concentration or major
was in charge of the curriculum."[2] While the pattern varies, general education requirements are most usually fulfilled through patterns of required
distribution with these distribution courses most frequently introductory departmental courses, i.e., courses introductory to the major. (They
are, in fact, perceived by many departments as recruitment devices for
the major.) In many instances, sample distribution patterns are "recommended" by the various major programs. As students are asked to make
increasingly early decisions, with respect to their major, the major determines both the shape and content of their general education courses. As
a result, major courses represent a disproportionately large part of most
students' baccalaureate programs, and electives are most frequently taken
within the chosen field of the major or in closely allied fields (these latter,
often stipulated by the major).

If the major has rarely been defended on intellectual grounds, save
for vague appeals to "depth," whence cometh its power? The power of the
major is preeminently political for the major is coextensive with departments, whether at a university (where some attempt has been made to
provide them with a rationale) or in a college (where there appears to be
little justification). Because of this, any inquiry into the major begins
with the fact that, although there have been a variety of experiments, no

convincing alternative to the department as an organizing principle for academic affairs has gained assent.[3]

As with the major, so with departments: they have rarely been justified on educational grounds. They are a convenience, like zip codes, a way of sorting the mail, a mode of governance, an agreeable way of doing business. It is often conceded by even their strongest advocates that departments lack intellectual coherence. But if this is true, we are entitled to ask some questions. What has become of the putative rationale for the major, if departments lack coherence? What could it possibly mean to experience a depth of incoherence? It is one thing to plumb the depths of clear water; it is surely another matter to muck about in a swampy ooze.

When we reflect on our daily lives as citizens of the academy, we see the fraudulence of the claim that the department is an adequate mapping of human knowledge and inquiry. Many of us find our most proximate colleagues in other departments, yet, through the hegemony of the major, we deny this to our students. It is as if we were compelled to confine our research and inquiry only to those areas of the library arbitrarily assigned "to us" by the Dewey Decimal or Library of Congress system. Through the major's domination of the curriculum we often confine our students' to such an odd set of limitations, those areas of inquiry arbitrarily assigned to a given major by faculty action and academic tradition. The library, at least, pretends no status for its system other than ease in retrieval. Our system confers status. Perhaps most explicitly when we confer a degree (despite all formulae) in the name of a major.

In most cases, departments and majors lack coherence because they are neither subject matters nor disciplines. Rather than the principled stipulation of a domain of inquiry (a perfectly legitimate endeavor), they are the result of a series of gentlemen's agreements. Take, as an example, a department or a major in English literature—frequently one of the larger and most politically self-conscious units on campus. Scholars in English employ a host of methods, not one of which is unique to their field of inquiry, most of which are shared with the majority of other departments in the humanities and, increasingly, with the social sciences as well. Nor is there any coherent limit, any modesty, to their domain. Almost anything printed from left to right in roman type may be taught: from Greek tragedies to world literature; from myth to mysticism; psychoanalytic theory, social anthropology, popular literature, technical texts.

But there is a *sine qua non* about which they are uncommonly clear: the number of slots they are entitled to. The formula is well-known to any academic administrator. The ideal department of English will have twenty-five slots, divided thusly: Literature from the fifteenth to twentieth century, five slots; double that for England and America to total ten slots; and, of course, prose and poetry for each of these must be considered, making twenty slots. Add Chaucer, Shakespeare, or drama and creative writing and the department is up to twenty-three places. Be avant-garde and include black literature, cinema, or some such and you have a staff of twenty-five. What is disciplinary about this? What are the principles of coherence? What could depth possibly mean in such a context?

The frequent answer, that such programs are, in fact, interdisciplinary will not do. Interdisciplinary work presumes intact, hard-edged disciplines. The discovery of an area of inquiry, a subject matter, that might fruitfully be addressed by more than a single discipline is an enterprise (Venn-diagram like) always and necessarily narrower than either discipline's full domain.[4]

Lacking principled stipulation, most majors are incoherent. This is especially noticeable at the middle range. While the first course is frequently a well-organized survey, and the last course an individualized research project, what comes in-between is political rather than substantive: a course with each of the major professors, or the like. Most majors, at their middle range, are miniaturized distribution requirements, and fall prey to the same criticism of such requirements at a more general level. It would be difficult to articulate in most instances in what respects they bring study in depth.[5]

Depending upon definition, it is possible to test for depth in such courses. If depth be defined in the context of the total curriculum, then depth must have a relation to the general education courses. That is to say, one could test a course in the major for its explicit reference to and use of general education courses, and for its capacity to "come at" the same or analogous materials in a more complex, "deeper" fashion. If depth be defined in terms of a particular subject matter, then one would expect that textbooks would be rarely used and that the seminar format would prevail. That students would be exposed to primary materials, to genuine areas of uncertainty and debate within the discipline. The majority of syllabi I have reviewed fail these two, most obvious tests.

Finally, there is what is not taught because it is not well captured by the departmental major. For example, when the intellectual history of this century is written, it will probably lift up the linguistic turn and the enormous influence thinking about language-as-such has had on most areas of inquiry in the humanities and social sciences (indeed, the linguistic turn has called into question many of the traditional borders between the humanities and the social sciences) as well in the biological and physical sciences. But where is this turn taught and studied in our colleges? Glimmers of it are found in a variety of programs, but its liberating and challenging aspects are rarely experienced. Its depth remains unplumbed by our students because it has been diffused (and defused).

One cannot think about a major except in the context of some overall conception of the baccalaureate degree. In the staggering diversity of colleges there are a multitude of spatial arrangements—ways in which blocks of courses are organized—but there is uniformity and harsh limitation of time.[6] Regardless of the academic calendar employed, there are almost always less than one hundred hours of course time in a yearlong course, and regardless of what we do, we must do it in the equivalent of four years. It is with this bureaucratic fact that thinking about the curriculum must begin. For, under these conditions, everything cannot be taught, nothing (so long as the baccalaureate degree is properly conceived as a terminal degree and not merely as preparation for postbaccalaureate studies or careers) needs to be taught. Thinking about the components of an undergraduate education is an occasion for institutional choice, for articulate and self-conscious selection.

I take as a corollary to this that each thing taught or studied is taught or studied not because it is "there," but because it is an example, an exempli gratia of something fundamental that may serve as a precedent for further interpretation and understanding. By providing an arsenal of skills and paradigms from which to reason, that which may first appear to be strange or novel can become intelligible.

Given this: that each thing which is taught is taught by way of an example and that the curriculum is an occasion for institutional choice, then the primary choice is, What shall the things taught exemplify? This ought to be explicit in every academic endeavor, at every level of the curriculum.

If this be so, then the curricular choices, the choice of what each component exemplifies, ought to be a conscious faculty decision which may well presume other modes of faculty governance than the present federation of departments. The implication is that these goals are public, that they may be tested by the faculty as a whole, rather than owned by some subset. For it will be the goals and choices which generate the components of the curriculum, much as one may design a course by starting with the final examination.

To these matters of choice and exemplification, no single answer can be given. These must remain institutional choices which fit each institution's peculiar ecology. But we may demand that they be articulated, and tested for, and that the goals be explicitly built into every course of study and not left for accidental discovery by a student. Students ought not to be asked to organize and integrate what the faculty will not.[7] Distribution requirements—whether at the level of general education or the middle range of the major, violate these two injunctions at will.

What has been suggested so far might be seen as the irreducible minimum for a baccalaureate program to argue that it had a curriculum, and indicates the ways in which the hegemony of the major, by its self-evident character, has deflected attention from such matters. The argument has been in terms of academic processes and governance, but behind such a view stands a set of presuppositions concerning knowledge. I expose these now as an example of the sort of debate that ought to go on among a faculty which takes seriously its responsibility for curriculum, but not as the necessary presuppositions for assuming such responsibilities or for questioning the major.

The world is not "given." It is not simply "there." We constitute it by acts of interpretation. (Some of which, in their characteristic modes and strategies, might well be organizing principles for domains of knowledge in the academy.) Above all, we constitute the world by speech, by memory, and by judgment. It is by an act of human will, through projects of language and history, through symbols and memory, that we fabricate the world and ourselves. But there is a double sense to the word "fabrication." It means both "to build" and "to lie." Education comes to life in the moment of tension generated by this duality. For, though we have no other means than language for treating with the world, words and symbols are not the same as that which they seek to name and describe. Though we have no other recourse than to memory and precedent if the world is not to be endlessly novel and, hence, forever unintelligible, the fit is never exact, nothing is ever quite the same. What is required at this point of tension is the trained capacity for judgment, for appreciating and criticizing the relative adequacy and insufficiency of any proposal of language and of memory.

This quest for the powers and skills of informed judgment, for the dual capacities of appreciation and criticism might well stand as the explicit goal of every level of the college curriculum. The difficult enterprise of making interpretive decisions and facing up to their full consequences ought to inform each and every course, each and every object of study.

The fundamentals of a college education, from such a viewpoint, are decisions between interpretations, the skills attendant upon the understanding of particular interpretations, and the ability to translate one interpretation in terms of another. Above all, they are that which leads to the capacity for argumentation, and, therefore, to responsible judgments. *Baccalaureate education is argument about interpretations.*

Of course there will be generalities and particulars. Knowledge is always knowledge about something in terms of something else. This is the act of interpretation; this is the generator of argument. But it is these acts, rather than the "somethings," which comprise the goal of the curriculum.

From such a view, there is even more pressure for articulate faculty argument and choice. For surely we must be able to undertake these endeavors before we dare to claim that we are teaching choice to our students. But one can dissent from these presuppositions, and yet affirm the consequences.

For, as faculty, we are not passive, we do not merely report and transmit what is there (indeed, much of what we teach was not there until we began to teach, to inquire, to interpret it). This implies a willingness, as a faculty, to experience the delicious terror of freedom and the awesome, concomitant exhilaration of decision.

Let us have an end to passing off our responsibility to our students and their high schools. It is not the careerism of our students that has disfigured liberal learning, but our own, and that of our colleagues. It is not the deficiencies of secondary education students that has weakened liberal learning, but rather that of graduate schools, dominated, as they are, by departmental concerns, which train our faculty and which we, rather than local school boards, control.

The question of the major and the status of the baccalaureate degree is a matter of faculty assuming their chartered responsibility. The convenience and political advantages of domination by the major have obscured this task. If the faculty does not make itself publicly and articulately responsible to itself, it will be made responsible to some other body. That would be a high cost, indeed.

Notes

Change: The Magazine of Higher Learning 15, no. 5 (July/August 1983): 12–15. ©
Taylor and Francis, http://www.informaworld.com. Reprinted by permission.
Excerpts from this article were later reprinted in "The Best of *Change*: 25th
Anniversary Issue," *Change* 26 (1994).

1. These issues are framed in a wider context in "Re-Forming the
    Undergraduate Curriculum," esp. 97–99.—Ed.
2. Frederick Rudolph, *Curriculum: A History of the Undergraduate Course of
    Study Since 1636* (San Francisco: Jossey-Bass, 1977), 248.
3. On the intellectual incoherence and political threat of departments, and
    related matters, see also "Connections," 55–56; "Religious Studies: Whither
    (Wither) and Why?" 69 passim; "'Religion' and 'Religious Studies':
    No Difference At All," 81–82; and "Re-Forming the Undergraduate
    Curriculum," 107–108.—Ed.
4. See the more extended discussion of disciplinary self-definition and
    Stephen Toulmin in "To Double Business Bound," 144–147.—Ed.
5. On the need for a proper, coherent "middle range," see also "Here and
    Now: Prospects for Graduate Education," 41–42.—Ed.
6. Compare these next pages, on time limits, coverage, and fabrication,
    with "The Introductory Course: Less Is Better," 13–15 and "Puzzlement,"
    125–128.—Ed.
7. Smith's "iron law": see "Re-Forming the Undergraduate Curriculum,"
    94.—Ed.

For Further Study

In reflecting on the major, I have been helped by the following:

Carnegie Foundation for the Advancement of Teaching. *Missions of the College
    Curriculum: A Contemporary Review with Suggestions.* San Francisco: Jossey-Bass,
    1977. Esp. 189–99.

Levine, Arthur. *Handbook on Undergraduate Curriculum.* San Francisco: Jossey-
    Bass, 1978. Esp. 28–53.

Levine, Arthur, and John Weingart. *Reform of Undergraduate Education.* San
    Francisco: Jossey-Bass, 1973.

McHenry, Dean E., et al. *Academic Departments: Problems, Variations, and Alternatives.*
    San Francisco: Jossey-Bass, 1977.

Rudolph, Frederick. *Curriculum: A History of the Undergraduate Course of Study Since
    1636.* San Francisco: Jossey-Bass, 1977.

Puzzlement

I LIKE THE WORD *puzzlement*, not only because it has a delicious sound, but also because, fittingly, of all the words I might have brought to this first oblique sally at my assigned topic (which is, in fact, the "Aims of Education"), it is the only one which my etymological dictionaries agree possesses "origin obscure." If the word *puzzle/puzzlement* is itself a puzzle (at least as to pedigree), then puzzlement about puzzlement has been doubled, and we have found just the sort of target one might contemplate aiming education at.

Perhaps, in part, this compounding of confusion may be blamed on the fact that I chose a relatively modern word, born in England, rather than appealing to the classier antique language of *paideia*. Might I have played my part more successfully if I had begun by quoting Aristotle, "For it is owing to their wonder that men both now begin and first began to philosophize" (*Metaphysics* 982b), or the earlier Platonic dictum, "This sense of wonder is the mark of the philosopher. Philosophy, indeed, has no other origin" (*Theatetus* 155D)? Perhaps...but here, as elsewhere, my sense of Greek has been altered by living too much in the world of New Testament and *koine* discourse where words built on *thauma/thaumazein*, especially in the Gospel of Mark with reference to the obdurate disciples, must often be translated by words such as *stupefied*, and, in more cases than not, result in paralysis and speechlessness. *Thauma*-terminology, from such a perspective, might best be rendered, "to be struck dumb"— surely an anti-educational stance. Latent in *wonder* is extreme passivity.

Concealed in the passage from Aristotle's *Metaphysics* from which I quoted one line, is a second Greek term which, at first glance, appears more promising: *aporia* together with its host of related terms (mixing Greek and English): *aporetic, aporime, aporema, diaporesis*. It is a term that first occurs in Pindar and carries the root sense of having no door, no exit or entrance, no possibility of passage. One definition (Edward Phillips) of *aporime* comes close to what I want, "difficult but not impossible, e.g., squaring a circle"; however the range suggests that, here too, paralysis is the dominant latent notion. Again, New Testament Greek makes this manifest. *Aporia* in Luke 21:25 must be translated by a word such as *anxiety*, followed as it is by "men fainting with fear," while *aporeo* carries, at the least, the sense of uncertainty, more strongly in Acts 25:20 where the Revised Standard Version properly translates, "Being at a loss how to investigate these problems...." Once more, an anti-educational stance. No ... the Greeks did not have a very satisfactory word for it. What I want is indicated by any dictionary of synonyms which tries to locate *puzzlement*: "puzzle implies presenting an intricate, difficult, *but solvable* problem" (*American Heritage Dictionary*). Accept this as a first, provisional definition of the educational enterprise.

Having thus dispatched the question of education, let me turn to an equally oblique and similarly provisional sally at the second definitional task presented by my assignment, that provoked by the word *aims*. Here, a dictionary of synonyms enlarges rather than reduces the problem. Locating aim within a range including *intention, intent, purpose, design, aim, end, object, objective, goal*, one dictionary stipulates *aim's* differentiating characteristic as implying "a clear definition of something that one hopes to effect and a direction of one's efforts or energies to its attainment" (*Webster's New Dictionary of Synonyms*). This is double jeopardy indeed! If education is to have as an aim a "clear definition of something one hopes to effect," then the accurate pluralism of *aims* suggests the scope of the problem, let alone the difficulty of attaining of such ends. Indeed, pluralism is here, as so often in academic discourse, a charitable term. Educational institutions (read the opening paragraphs of their public literature) when they speak of their aims are better characterized by words such as cacophony. Collectively, they are Babel, producing a motley list of doubtlessly worthy goals, impossibly and often heedlessly combined. Checked at the outset, you came close to receiving an exceedingly short address. However, my eye was caught by the etymology of *aim*. Most modern dictionaries agree that it was derived from the Latin through an Old French verb meaning *to guess* (related to the English, *to estimate*). Some older dictionaries argue for another pedigree, likewise from Latin through an Old French verb meaning *to value* (related to the English, *to esteem*). Indeed, both the redoubtable Skeat and the magisterial *OED* declare, with a touch of indignation, that there has been a "confusion...in the word *aim*, probably two verbs have been confounded." I prefer the modern derivation (although we shall have occasion to recall the older). I glory in the fact that there is "confusion," disagreement, and argument built into the history of the English word *aim*. Consonant with this, I propose a provisional revision of my topic. Rather than "Aims of Education" it should be "Guesses about Education."

Combining these two initial sallies, what I want to invite you to engage in this evening is guessing about the processes of posing intricate, difficult but solvable problems. To do so, let us make a fresh (but no less oblique) beginning.

In her novel, *Precious Bane*, published in 1924, the regional British writer, Mary Webb, has her heroine exclaim in Shropshire dialect: "It made me gladsome to be getting some education, it being like a big window opening." How many of our students, I wonder, would say the same? For how many of them, rather, would the word *education* carry the sort of connotations suggested by a sadistic contraption called an "education chair" as described in the *Atlantic Monthly* for 1865: "[it] compelled girls to sit bolt upright...by way of keeping their shoulders flat and strengthening their spines." If we believe education to be, above all, "gladsome," we certainly keep it to ourselves. A recent survey (1980) of college recruitment materials and catalogs revealed the following as the stated goals of more than three hundred liberal arts colleges:

70% listed intellectual development
69% listed development of a student's human potential
58% listed job preparation
44% listed the acquisition of, or study of, values
40% listed broad exposure to varied fields of knowledge
40% listed development of religious values
37% listed training in basic skills
30% listed providing the foundations for life-long learning
29% listed developing the capacity for critical thinking
28% listed enhancing capacities for creativity
22% listed preparation for citizenship
21% listed cultivation of aesthetic sensibility
19% listed training in research
18% listed development of specialized knowledge
16% listed exposure to other cultures

and so on, down to the utterly idiosyncratic, the majority of one. This list accords well with a similar survey from 1977, although the latter found more emphasis on preparation for "fruitful leisure," on "an understanding of the basic principles for cultivating physical and mental health," and on what was termed "consumer efficiency," defined as "sound choice of values relating to style of life." As I read through the Babel of either list, I find no one insisting on something primarily "gladsome," something like "having fun," more particularly that sort of fun associated with the intellect and its all but limitless capacity for the analogous activities of experimentation, argumentation, imagination, and "fooling around."

Perhaps this is not surprising. Such publications reflect all too faithfully the institutions which they serve. By and large they are innocent of any joyous (or challenging) educational thoughts because their constituencies are bereft of the same. The literature rarely performs its central educational task, the articulation to the potential student of the essential differences between high school and college-level work, because their institutions have rarely reflected on the same (except, perhaps, to complain about their students' secondary education). Despite the myth, held firmly by the majority of college faculties and writ large in William J. Bennett's recent spleenful report, this widespread institutional malaise was *not* the result of the faculty, in the sixties, giving the curriculum over to the students. It was rather the result of the faculty, in the sixties, giving the curriculum over to themselves in their new guise, not as teachers chiefly engaged in playfully enlarging the minds and perspectives of the young ("it being like a big window opening"), but as recruitment representatives for the several disciplines and academic professions, engaged in focusing the minds and perspectives of the students so as to produce—quixotically, despite the actual vocational plans of the vast majority of their students— clones of themselves.

I might have sought to engage you in the correction of a Greek text from the third century. I have always thought that old Diogenes Laertius, in his *Lives of the Philosophers*, got it wrong. He reports that when Aristotle was asked how the educated differ from the uneducated, the sage responded: "as much as the living from the dead." I have long suspected that what Aristotle actually said, with just such a figure as Diogenes in mind, was "as much as the lively from the deadly bores." I may note that I am encouraged in so altering the text by the fact that the leading manuscript of the *Lives*, the thirteenth-century Codex Barbonicus, Manuscript Greek III B 29 in the National Library at Naples, was written by a scribe who, according to its most prominent editor, "obviously knew no Greek." However, I failed to arrange for a projector, and so I must fall back to an alternative strategy. I take as my proof text for our inquiry a narrative I first learned years ago as a Yiddish vaudeville routine. It is a tale-type that has many variants within the complex world of Jewish humor, but one which I have also, more recently, found in a medieval Spanish Christian text and in a Japanese Zen version. It goes something like this:

Moses came before Pharaoh and said, "Let my people go." Pharaoh, like a good colonial administrator, answered him, "I'd like to, but your people are too dumb to survive off of the reservation. But I'll tell you what I'll do. You bring me your wisest man, and I'll question him." So Moses goes out and grabs the first Jew he happens to meet, whose name was Abe [the name is always Abe in such stories] and brings him before Pharaoh, and the following dialogue ensues. Pharaoh raises his hand; Abe raises his fist. Pharaoh puts up two fingers; Abe puts up one. Pharaoh takes out an egg; Abe takes out an apple. With this, Pharaoh, obviously agitated, cries out, "Stop! I need no more! This is the wisest man I have ever met, wiser than all my sages and magicians. I'm convinced. Your people may go." Abe, being no fool, quickly leaves, but Moses stays and addresses Pharaoh. "I don't understand. What went on?" Pharaoh replies, "Such wisdom I have never seen. I said to him that the world was flat and he said no it's round. I said that there were many gods, but he said there was only one. I said to him that the world emerged from an egg, he said no, it evolved from a seed."

Moses then goes outside and catches up with Abe. Still puzzled, he asks him, "Abe, what went on in there?" Abe replies, "That son of a bitch Pharaoh. I said to him no matter what he decreed, we'd leave anyway. He said, we'll stop you. I said, we'll fight. He said if we thought we could win we were jackasses. I said, 'up yours.' Then he saw who he was dealing with and decided to be friends so...he showed me his lunch and I showed him mine."

It is almost a shame to ruin a good story by insisting on drawing a lesson from it, but I shall persevere. That which is "other," be it the world, other folk, our own past, or what have you, is like the major activity in the story. It sends enigmatic signs at us and our job is to interpret them, to translate them into our language as best we can. This is what both

Pharaoh and Abe did, and their respective interpretations, though very different, are each thoroughly satisfying. The interesting figure for us in the story is Moses (who serves as the paradigm for liberal learning, especially in the human sciences). He has seen the signs, he has heard both interpretations and now his job is to translate the signs as well as the interpretations, and to decide between the alternative interpretations, to combine or reduce one to the other, or to propose yet a third interpretation of his own. It is, when you stop to think about it, a crazy endeavor, one in which not everything is possible, but one in which there can never, ever, be certainty. It is an undertaking more closely akin to play than to work. It is an undertaking which most closely resembles that which ought to occupy every college classroom.

The difference between college and high school level work, that which ought to be an explicit object of reflection in higher education, lies primarily in the attitude towards words and discourse. In college, words are no longer thought to be expressive of things (in philosophical terms, they are no longer real), they are no longer vocabularies to be mastered (30 *Minutes a Day*) or to be judged by the degree to which they conform to something "out there." In college, it is we who master words. Rather than evaluate the relationship of words to things, we evaluate the relationship of words to other words and to other acts of human imagination. It is a process that has many names, but, above all, it is known as argument. For it is argument that marks the distinctive mode of speech which characterizes college. This faculties need to remember, this students need to know. [I feel this so strongly that I have long wished that each college would send its admitted students, before they matriculate, a book such as Jack Meiland's *College Thinking* which speaks directly, in its opening chapters, to such matters. Such would be a proper orientation to college-level work. I feel this so strongly that I tell the students in each of my classes that they will get an automatic *F* if they write in their papers phrases such as "merely a semantic difference," "merely verbal," "merely symbolic." For there is little else available to the human intellect but symbols. There is no other way of doing our work in that laboratory which is the classroom except by being scrupulously attentive to words and to matters such as semantic difference.]

Despite what we may sometimes claim, in contradistinction to secondary education, college is not a learning experience. Planaria, bees, mice, perhaps even machines, can all learn. That is to say, they can process information and retain it. They can discern repetitive, significant patterns on the basis of past experience. They can undertake efficient and effective action on the basis of such information and patterns. And, if these fail, in some sense they can innovate. But no other being than humankind, as far as we know, can argue and, therefore, be educated in the sense I am using the term. For argument is not based on the world as it is, but rather on what the world might imply. It is the world as refracted, no longer *the* world, but rather *our* world—a world of significance, of interpretation, of translation, and, therefore, of argument. It is a relentlessly social world, for significance, interpretation, and argument are impossible without fellow human beings. Even as words they seem strangely naked without their attendant prepositions. It is this "second environment," the social, in contradistinction to the "natural," that is the arena and object of education. For this reason, collegiate education (as its very name indicates) is always political and, therefore, must be always undertaken in a corporate setting.

Behind such an understanding of education stands a set of presuppositions, of guesses if you please, concerning knowledge and the way of the world. Chief among these is that the world is not given, it is not simply "there." We constitute it by acts of interpretation. We constitute it by activities of speech and memory and judgment. It is by an act of human will, through projects of language and history, through words and memory, that we fabricate the world and ourselves. But there is a double sense to the word *fabrication*. It means both to build and to lie.[1] Education comes to life at the moment of tension generated by this duality. For, though we have no other means than language for treating with the world, words are not, after all, the same as that which they signify. Though we have no other recourse than to memory, to precedent, if the world is not to be endlessly novel and, hence, forever unintelligible, the fit is never exact, nothing is ever quite the same. What is required at this point of tension is the trained capacity for judgment, for appreciating and for criticizing the relative adequacy and insufficiency as well as the implications of any proposal of language and memory. This training is the work of education.

All this has been put with uncommon elegance in the lapidary formulation of that late gifted Argentinian author, Borges, a sentence that ought to be placed at the entrance to every college and university: "Reality may avoid the obligation to be interesting, but hypotheses may not." To translate Borges into a more prosaic terminology, this difference is caused by the fact that we do not argue with the world, but with each other. We argue with one another's hypotheses, proposals, and interpretations, with the way each construes the world and its parts.

I do not know what came into your mind when you heard Borges's word, "interesting." Although, for me, it is, perhaps, the most solemn and powerful word I can utter, it has suffered grievous banalization. We say, "How interesting," when we really mean, "Ho hum." "How was Smith's talk?" "Oh, it was interesting," constitutes a prime example of what is meant by damning with faint praise. To find something interesting is often no more than what a Frenchman means when he finds it "very amusing" (*très amusant*).

Such a notion of interesting is appropriate to that genteel social world constituted by gossip that was once characteristic of the liberal arts college conceived of as a finishing school.[2] In this context, what is interesting is the unexpected, the slightly out of place. "Is he handsome?" "No...but he has an interesting face." "Isn't it interesting who the Dean was with at lunch?"

This notion of interesting reminds me of those sixteenth- and seventeenth-century cabinets of curiosities—direct ancestors of "Ripley's Believe It or Not," more remote ancestors of our contemporary museums. The cabinets displayed a hotchpotch of exotica, arranged in pleasing, symmetrical aesthetic patterns. Thus sea shells, coins, fossils, a coconut, a shrunken head, a dried sea horse, a mermaid's hand, an oriental dagger, and a "fragment of the Tower of Babel" (to quote one seventeenth-century catalog) would be juxtaposed, one to the other, with no reason except that they catch the fancy of the spectator. Note that, with the possible exception of the mermaid's hand and the fragment from Babel (which were genuine artifacts, merely mislabeled), everything in such a collection was "real." The objects were factual, but they were meaningless, they were insignificant in the strict sense of the word, for they told no story, they raised no questions, they demanded no decisions. They were inarticulate, or, at best, they provided an occasion for gossip. "See that...*très amusant!*"

What I have described is the sense of *interesting* as trivialized in common discourse. However, there is another understanding, one closer to the original meaning of the word which has been continued in the current legal and commercial term *interest*. It is this sense of *interesting*, rather than the gossipy, that is appropriate to the discourse of a contemporary college. For, in this understanding, things that are interesting, things that become objects of interest, are things in which one has a stake, things which place one at risk, things for which one is willing to pay some price, things which make a difference. When a book, an idea, an object is found to be interesting in this sense, it is not because it titillates, but rather because it challenges, because it exacts some cost. Ultimately, it is interesting because it challenges the way in which one has construed the world and because, therefore, it may compel one to change.

In contradistinction to the objects displayed in the cabinets of curiosities, such objects of interest require articulation. They call forth speech and discourse, not gossip. They provoke argument. As such, they cannot be allowed to stand alone as isolated specimens or to be arranged in superficially pleasing patterns. They must be integrated into a coherent view of the world, or they must challenge previous proposals of coherence and integration. Indeed, things may be most interesting when they are capable of being construed in a variety of ways and when one may tot up the gain or loss of each proposal. Things are *interesting* in the fullest sense of the word when they exemplify, when they signify, when they criticize, when they entail—in short, when they are consequential.

What we labor at together in college is the production of individuals who know not only that the world is far more complex than it first appears, but also that, therefore, interpretative decisions must be made, decisions of judgment which entail real consequences for which one must take responsibility and from which one may not flee by the dodge of disclaiming expertise. This ultimately political quest for paradigms, for the acquisition of the powers and skills of informed judgment, for the dual capacities of appreciation and criticism, might well stand as the explicit goal of every level of the college curriculum. The difficult art of making interpretative decisions and facing up to their consequences ought to inform each and every course, each and every object of study. This is the work of education, it is also the work of the world and of life. Let students and the public and, above all, the faculty be told this clearly. This is the only sort of work for which college trains. It is more than enough.

We should not participate in courses in the natural or the human sciences in order, primarily, to train would-be practitioners, nor to provide a smattering of information to enliven future cocktail parties or produce better consumers of the evening news. As a teacher, I do not care if, months after some course, a student no longer recalls what particular thing Aristotle or Durkheim said, if he or she no longer remembers what a virtual proton is thought to "be" according to some version of perturbation theory, but I would insist that each student gain some sense of the way in which the world is construed by each of the major domains of human knowledge and some sense of the arguments between them as well as what each entails for human life. What if man and the world are as the humanities or the social sciences or the biological or physical sciences would have it? What then? What would it be like to inhabit such a world? What modes of speech would one have to master in order to translate one's individual perception of the world and one's humanity into such proposals? What modes of speech would one have to master in order to translate these rival proposals into each other's terms? In each of the central arguments between the major modes of human knowledge one is confronted with a choice as to citizenship, with a choice as to the implications and lineaments of possible worlds in which one might choose to dwell. The issue for education is to describe the topographies and consequences of such interpretative worlds and to learn how to negotiate, how to make responsible decisions between them. From such a perspective, if I were asked to define education in college, it would be that it is essentially concerned with argumentation. Education is argument about interpretations.

Perhaps I have been too hortatory. I have largely preached you a sermon, one not innocent of curricular implications, but one that may well be judged not practical enough to justify the extraction of as much as twenty-five cents a minute, at some institutions, as the cost of participating in the game, as the price of fussing and fooling around. (There is nothing like the current annual cycle of tuition-rate increases to drive playfulness from the college classroom, leading to the absurd paradox that the more we charge, the less truly educational we become.) So, let me take another tack.

It is both wonderful and unaccountable, perhaps even comic or crazy, that sometimes our playful imagination, our arguments about and mental construals of the world turn out to have real consequences. One thinks of a Mendeleyev who, by sheer force of logic and an uncommon faith in order, was not only capable of organizing all known elements, but, in his revised periodic table of 1871, left gaps for those elements not yet known which he, nevertheless, accurately described. Each of these was subsequently discovered within the next twenty years, only because he imagined them. Did he ever feel like Peter Vierick's poet:

> Not priest but clown, the shuddering sorcerer
> is more astounded than his rapt applauders:
> "Then all these props and Easters of my stage
> came true? But I was joking all the time!"

The moral we ought to derive from such a seductive example is not that the scientists were "right" (this time) whatever that might mean. The moral ought to be that which I take as one of the prime rules of collegiate education: no one can be wrong. It's a rule similar to that formula intoned by generations of math teachers extending back to grade school: "Hand in your worksheets along with your answers, because it is not the answers that count, but how you got them." It is a sentiment echoed by one of the great mathematicians, Carl Friedrich Gauss, when he wrote, "I have my answers, I do not know how I am to arrive at them."

I remember well the stimulus which first got me thinking about becoming a teacher. It was an article, some thirty years ago, in the *New York Times Magazine*, about disciplinary problems in the New York City high schools. A sidebar pointed out that students so labeled were not always lacking in intelligence and gave the following example. A teacher asked, on an exam, how students would determine the height of a very tall building using only a barometer. They were meant, I suppose, to employ the formula that pressure decreases 3.5 millibars for every 30 meters of ascent, but two students wrote a somewhat different sort of answer. One stated that he would go to the top of the building, throw the barometer off, and count how long it took to reach the ground. The other student wrote that if it were a very expensive barometer, he'd use it to bribe the superintendent of the building to tell him how tall it was. Both were suspended as disciplinary problems. I thought then (and I still do now) that each deserved the adolescent equivalent of a Nobel Prize. The example made plain what teaching ought not to be; it suggested as well, although only by indirection, what it might be and that could be fun.

To put this another way, allow me to repeat a suggestion I made in an after-dinner speech to the annual meeting of the Midwest Regional Association of the College Board. If the SATs are to be truly prophetic of college-level work rather than merely retrospective, then their present insistence on singularity, on the "right answer," is wholly inappropriate. It is irrelevant, misleading, and (worse yet) it is boring. My fantasy as to the proper test for college-level work would be an examination in which each one of the listed alternatives was stated at the outset to be plausible and in which evaluation depended solely on one's arguments for *each* of the options.

It is, perhaps, inappropriate for a professor of the humanities to appear to be picking on the sciences, so let me come closer to home where the same sorts of issues recur. The professor of English who recently marked a student "wrong" for interpreting the line in Emily Dickinson—"Till Seraphs swing their snowy hats"—as clouds rather than snow, hence reading the poem, "I Taste a Liquor Never Brewed" as being about death rather than seasonal change, is exemplary of the type. Interpretation, like translation (the linguistic model on which the humanities is finally based), inhabits the playful world of the in-between. It can never be right or wrong, true or mistaken. It can only be more or less persuasive depending on the arguments and their implications.

Even at supposedly more sophisticated levels, the humanities all too often exhibit the fallacy of misplaced seriousness. Claude Lévi-Strauss is surely one of the seminal minds of the twentieth century. His works stand as a monument to what a scholar can achieve while fooling around. He persistently invites his readers, among other things, to enjoy watching his mind at work, uncovering unexpected relationships, following out chains of associations. It is for this reason that, at Chicago, we teach his most accessible book to our freshmen in our core. That book, *La pensée sauvage* (*The Savage Mind*), was duly and dully translated and brought out by my university's press. The cover is chaste, featuring only the author's name and the book's title, conforming to some staid image of an academic classic and thereby missing, at the outset, a central theme in Lévi-Strauss's work. The original French edition, by Lévi-Strauss's command, had a picture of a flowering plant on the cover because *la pensée sauvage*, in French, means both savage mind and wild pansy (*Viola tricolor*). It was a joke, but it was also indicative of the very heart of Lévi-Strauss's intellectual enterprise. We were not meant to reduce the ambiguity that gave rise to the visual pun, to choose, in terms of the story given earlier, either Pharaoh's or Abe's interpretation. Both were to be held simultaneously as a stimulus to thought. How is the mind like a flower? It is on such puzzles that the human sciences are founded, negotiating constantly between shifting perspectives of like and unlike to some cognitive end.

Within the wordy world of the human sciences, the special form this negotiation takes is a cognate of the general educational principle, "no one can be wrong," as expressed in the old Latin tag, "Nothing human is foreign to me." It is this assertion which is the ultimate ground of, but also in some sense the pragmatic justification for, the endeavor of humanistic education as discourse with and translation of the "other," whether that other be conceived as spatially or temporally different.

It is this assertion which stands as the utter refutation of one of the most depressing public confessions that I have read, Meg Greenfield's Christmas column in *Newsweek* two years ago. She wrote:

> There are those great flashing boards and clocks and monitors one
> reads about that periodically record...some cataclysmic moment

that has been reached. The national debt has hit a trillion! The population has gone over 200 million! Things like that. The big board began flashing for me again last week. It was 7:25 a.m. (EST) on Friday the 16th of December, to be precise. I was deep in the morning paper when suddenly the thing went off. "Bingo! Gridlock! Whoopee!" it signaled in huge digital letters. "The news from abroad has finally become totally and irrevocably incomprehensible! Congratulations, America! Happy New Year, everyone!" You think I'm being frivolous or hysterical or both. Very well, I will tell you exactly what the daily news take had been at the point when the big board lit up. The Israeli army had helped to get 2,000 "Lebanese Christian militiamen" out of harm's way.... The battleship New Jersey had shelled "Syrian-backed Druse militia positions in the mountains."..."The fighting in Tripoli today was between fiercely anti-Syrian Muslim fundamentalist militiamen...and their longstanding pro-Syrian Muslim Alawite militia foes." You might as well give up; nothing you can say will convince me that you understand any better than either the American government...[or the Press] does who all these various warring elements are, let alone what they want.... Electronic miracles take us from place to place—Angola, Chad, Grenada—almost faster than our leaders can learn to pronounce their names. And we are living in a moment when a whole post-war system of political and economic arrangements seem to be up for revision, so that our role in all the global skirmishing is less clear to us. But that doesn't tell you who in the hell the Druse Progressive Socialist Party militia are or the Grenada New Jewel Movement. We are tourists everywhere affecting the role of natives. (*Newsweek* 12/23/83)

If it be true, as Greenfield claims, that "the news from abroad has finally become totally and irrevocably incomprehensible," then we are in deep trouble indeed. We are in trouble both as citizens and as individuals concerned with processes of education. For what it signals is an abdication of the difficult responsibility to interpret, the refusal to inhabit the uneasy world of the in-between.

In recent times, the paradigm of this refusal was the Iranian hostage crisis and the figure of the Ayatollah Khomeini. As I was teaching at the time in one of our Western civilization sequences (a term for me which includes both the ancient Near East and Islam), I decided to make the crisis the topic of my student's final class project. What if we began with the required principle, "Nothing human is foreign to me"? What consequences would flow from such an assertion? We agreed on the following:

1. We would have to assume at the outset that Khomeini was not insane.
2. Therefore, he must know that he cannot "win" (in our terms). That is to say, the hostages must ultimately be released.
3. The daily press gave us ample reason to assume that the conflict, as seen in Iran, was primarily symbolic. For example, the phone was answered at the captured embassy with the phrase, "United States synagogue of Satan." Let me add that the fact that a major resource was the daily press—and Ted Koppel—was crucial, not for its contemporaneity, but because it placed teacher and students on an equal footing with regard to data.
4. We ventured the hypothesis that Islam might be interpreted, as the Homeric Greeks we had studied, as what anthropologists term a "shame culture." This meant, among other things, that "face" would have to be preserved.
5. Therefore, the rational problem for Khomeini was how to win symbolically (i.e., how to preserve "face") even as he lets the hostages go.
6. The issue, after much discussion, seemed to be primarily a matter of timing.
7. We were able to determine, from readily available materials, that the date on which the embassy was stormed and the hostages taken was a deeply symbolic date for immediate Iranian history. On November 4, 1977, the son of Khomeini was killed (it was widely believed by the U.S.-backed Shah's secret police). On November 4, 1978, there were demonstrations commemorating the event at the University at Teheran during which thirty-six students were killed. On November 4, 1979, Iranian students captured the embassy and took sixty American hostages. Given the first two events, the class argued that something like the third action was predictable.
8. This allowed our class to assume that the date of release would be likewise predictable, that it would be a symbolic date and one that would allow, as well, Khomeini to "save face."

Having agreed on this chain of reasoning, the class was divided in two. One group explored symbolic reasons for releasing prisoners in connection with religious practices. (This was stimulated by a student recalling the alleged Roman practice of freeing a prisoner during Passover in the gospel's Passion Narrative.) They found a widespread custom of releasing prisoners on the anniversary of a king's birth or accession to the throne. In some countries, it was at Christmas (following a symbolism of Christ as king); in the Soviet Union, this occurred on the anniversary of the Revolution. While not being able to prove this custom's presence in Islamic countries, they guessed that if it were followed, it would commemorate Muhammad's birthday. In our calendar, this occurs during the week of January 13–19. Therefore, in early May 1980, they predicted the release of the hostages as not occurring before the week of January 13–19, 1981.

The second group researched the religious calendar of Shiite Islam in order to determine dates of mythical events and ritual celebrations which might suggest a propitious time for release. They found a complex pattern, one celebrated and reenacted in Shiite myth and ritual and encoded in the calendar. While the details are too complex to rehearse here, suffice it to say that the most sacred period in the Shiite calendar begins with the anniversary of their founding martyr—their holiest day—and concludes, forty days later, with a feast of celebration—their second holiest day. This latter seemed most plausible. Again, the time period was the week of January 13–19 and so, in early May 1980, they predicted the release of the hostages as not occurring before January 13–19, 1981.

Once this synchronism was proposed, we went back to consider recent Iranian history. The fact that on January 16, 1979, the Shah was deposed (for the second and the last time) leaving behind the provisional government of Bakhtiar (soon to be superseded by Khomeini) made our guess seem all the more secure. As you may recall, we were slightly off. The agreement to release was announced during the predicted dates (January 16, 1981), but a last-minute change in the terms of the agreement by the American banks brought about a delay. This caused a shift in the symbolic date from an Iranian calendar to an American one: the hostages were released on January 20, the day of Ronald Reagan's inauguration, minutes after Carter was no longer president.

I have rehearsed this example with you at some length, not in order to boast of our prescience. It little matters whether we were right or wrong, or whether we had the right dates for the wrong reasons. What is important is that we risked interpretation, that we hazarded a guess, that we refused to accept the premise that "the news from abroad has become totally and irrevocably incomprehensible," and that we, thereby, comported ourselves as responsible citizens—of both the academy and the world. In so doing, we undertook what ought to be the routine work of a college course. For collegiate education depends on, and trains for, the capacity to assume, simultaneously, differing points of view in order to engage in the interpretative enterprise and to reach some consequential decision. It is here, in such an in-between, that guessing and valuing finally come together. At times, this process may produce the "right answers"; at times, our discussions and arguments will be frustrating and inconclusive; at times, we will appear to have wasted our time. None of these is an inappropriate outcome, each is the precondition of the other. For a college education is governed, above all else, by Alfred North Whitehead's dictum: "Seek simplicity and distrust it."

What we celebrate in college is not rectitude. What we honor, above all else, are playful acts of imagination in the sense stipulated by Wallace Stevens when he wrote, "Imagination is the power of the mind over the possibility of things." We are, together, in the joyous business of enabling such power. On its attainment much, including the future, depends. In the undertaking of this task we stand charged, students and faculty alike, by the words of an ancient teacher and sage: "If not by us, then by whom? If not now, then when?"

Notes

T. March, ed., *Interpreting the Humanities* (Princeton: The Woodrow Wilson National Fellowship Foundation, 1986), 53–67. Reprinted by permission of the Woodrow Wilson National Foundation (Princeton, New Jersey). A sensitive abridgement of this article, entitled "Playful Acts of Imagination," was published in *Liberal Education* 73 (1987): 14–20.

1. Compare the remarks on "fabrication" with "The Introductory Course: Less Is Better," 13–15 and "Why the College Major?" 116–117.—Ed.
2. On "liberal" and "servile" arts, see "Re-Forming the Undergraduate Curriculum," 94–96.—Ed.

Bibliography

Bennett, William J. *To Reclaim a Legacy: A Report on the Humanities in Higher Education*. Washington, DC: National Endowment for the Humanities, 1984.
Bourdieu, Pierre. "Systems of Education and Systems of Thought." *International Social Science Journal*, 19 (1967): 338–352.

Maxwell, W. David. "A Methodological Hypothesis for the Plight of the Humanities." *AAUP Bulletin*, 54 (1968): 78–84.

McPeck, John E. *Critical Thinking and Education*. New York: St. Martins Press, 1981.

Meiland, Jack W. *College Thinking: How to Get the Best Out of College*. New York: Signet/New American Library, 1981.

Perelman, Charles, and L. Obrechts Tyteca. *The New Rhetoric: A Treatise on Argumentation*. Notre Dame, IN: University of Notre Dame Press, 1969.

Rescher, Nicholas. *Dialectics*. Albany: State University of New York Press, 1977.

Smith, Jonathan Z. "Commentary: William J. Bennett's "To Reclaim a Legacy."" *American Journal of Education* 93, no. 4 (August 1985): 541–546.

Toulmin, Stephen. *Human Understanding, vol. 1, The Collective Use and Evolution of Concepts*. Princeton, NJ: Princeton University Press, 1972.

12

Towards Imagining New Frontiers

IN THE PAST two years, we have been presented with a series of dire reports on the state of education in America. The majority (thank God) have focused on secondary education, some half-dozen on collegiate education, one on the holy of holies—graduate education.[1] There is much that is of interest in these documents, in the commonalities that may be observed. Of greatest potential significance, expressed in different ways in the College Board report, the report of the American Association of State Colleges and Universities, the report of the Association of American Colleges, and others is a shift from a language of topics and subjects to a language of skills and capacities broadly understood. There is, as well, much that is disturbing in many of these reports. Most have been distinguished by their nostalgia, by their overwhelming sense that we know what we ought to do—and that we did it once—but that, in recent times, we have simply not been doing enough of it, or have been doing it ineffectively. By so comporting ourselves, we have, in the arresting words of one of these reports, placed our nation "at risk."[2]

I doubt this element in these reports. In expressing such nostalgia they seem to me, in many ways, to be rearguard actions, conservative backlashes to a new situation in which, perversely, the fault is placed on people (students, parents, teachers) for failing to appreciate and realize the traditional institutionalized goals of education rather than seizing this juncture as a promising new opportunity and subjecting the goals, themselves, to scrutiny. Each report differs from the others chiefly in when and where it locates the moment of sin. Each assumes that there has been an expulsion from the Garden, and that we ought to strive to return. None of the reports appears to entertain the more daring possibility, latent in the old Yahwist's text in Genesis and seized on by later Gnostic interpreters, that the serpent might be telling the truth after all, that the expulsion might not be a "Fall" but a new and valid creation. What is common to many of these reports is that the "new frontier" they envisage for education turns out to be the past.

Let me be blunt. The situation we find ourselves in and which we look forward to is new, and it is promising. It marks the culmination of a process that began after World War II with the G.I. Bill of Rights and which is now driven by the new demographics of college students—the putting to death of the original understanding of the meaning of the adjective, "liberal," in the liberal arts.[3] (Never mind the hoked-up redefinition, "liberal" means "liberating.") As the *OED* would have it, the initial distinction was between the "liberal arts" and the "servile arts," the former being those "worthy of a freeman, pertaining to persons of superior social status, i.e., a gentleman," the latter referring to the "trades." The *OED* goes on to illustrate the connotation of the word "liberal" in the "liberal arts" or "liberal education" with the following quotation from 1801: "Two centuries back, horse racing was conceived as a liberal pastime, practiced for pleasure not for profit." Liberal education was designed to benefit a small, fairly homogenous social class, with at least a modicum of wealth, a shared culture and worldview, which had secure future position or employment, and which looked forward to having considerable leisure time. The liberal arts were designed to enrich one's life after 5 p.m. Liberal learning was the acquisition of the civilized art of gossip.

Today, this understanding is both impossible and offensive. However, it persists all too often in our rhetoric and our consciousness. We can hear echoes of it each time we decry the professionalism of our students, every time we use code words or euphemisms to signal our discomfort with the lack of a shared worldview brought about by the increasing diversity of our students.

I take it as axiomatic that it is the task of components within our educational institutions, especially those preeminently committed to collegiate education such as honors programs, to experiment with this new situation rather than to construct sanctuaries in which to protect the last exemplars of a dying breed.

The task before us, then, is the celebration and utilization of attributes such as professionalism and diversity to educational ends. How might such experimentation proceed?

I would locate the heart of our common enterprise in the conflict of interpretations. It is this which distinguishes collegiate education from the notions of learning and transmission enshrined in secondary school curricula and in the older, passive view of liberal learning atavistically expressed in William J. Bennett's report on the humanities. (My fantasy would be a set of College Boards in which all of the proposed answers were correct, or, more properly speaking, plausible.[4]) The fundamentals of a collegiate liberal arts education are decisions between interpretations, the skills attendant upon the understanding of particular interpretations, and the ability to translate one interpretation in terms of another. Above all, they are that which leads to the capacity for argumentation—for that which leads to responsible decisions and the acceptance of consequences. Education is argument about interpretations.[5]

There are two aspects of such a position worth lifting out. The first is its recognition of pluralism. This implies that a central topic for collegiate discussion (cutting across all fields of inquiry) ought to be the issue of relativism. It is a question begged in most of our curricula; it should be a central component of the new liberal arts. Second, such a position suggests how much we have to learn from our often polemicized-against colleagues in professional and preprofessional programs. In the new frontier that opens before us, I doubt that the distinction between liberal/professional will continue to be of much substantive interest. We might find that sustained reflection on work itself will provide a major curricular focus, perhaps in conjunction with a variety of forms of practice. We are long overdue in our recognition that professional education embodies modes of knowledge that should be incorporated into our curricula, forms of inquiry which the traditional studies of liberal arts colleges and programs are the poorer for lacking. There are two in particular: decision making and the awareness of institutional matrices.

The first affects the issue of "critical inquiry"—much lifted up of late as the hallmark of liberal learning (indeed, recently mandated as a required component of college curricula by state legislatures such as California). It is one thing to strive to overcome our students' naive first readings, to lead our students to become aware of the conflict of interpretations; it is another thing to resist all decisions (there's always another point of view) and the acceptance of responsibility attendant on the making of decisions. For all the ambiguities and possibilities, for all the uncertainties and accidentalities, there arises a point when business commits to a decision, when law reaches a verdict, when medicine proffers a diagnosis—and their practitioners are trained, explicitly, to do so.

In the classroom as well as the Oval Office, there comes a point where "the buck stops here," and this is not just a position to be assumed, but a solemn responsibility to be trained for.

Nor are such enterprises of judgment undertaken in solitude. They are made in social contexts, as part of networks of differing perspectives and alternative interests, of varying pressures of rank, status, and power. We do our work in institutional contexts which we have all too readily factored out in traditional courses of liberal learning. (The contemporary biology student needs to know as much about the NSF as DNA—where in the curriculum is this sort of need addressed?)

Alongside relativism, the making of decisions and matters of institutional context constitute a second agendum for the new frontier of liberal education. I would hope that each college or program might take its institutional and corporate self as a laboratory in this endeavor.

As I talk with colleagues on the research frontier, it appears that there begins to be consensus on the lineaments of what might be termed the "new liberal arts." I am tempted to group these under the rubric of what one scholar has termed (with a somewhat different end in view) the "sciences of the artificial."

Pride of place among these emergent sciences, and hence the center of gravity for a new frontier would be the study of language itself. Language has become the new Queen of the Sciences, breaking down every traditional disciplinary barrier and contributing insight to a rich variety of theoretical endeavors. It has begun to make plain what culture is and the way in which it relates to the natural environment—the two foci of the educational enterprise.

Of the many other possible components of the "sciences of the artificial," I have time to single out only one—representation and visualization as among the most-ignored topics in the present curriculum and one that must be central in any projection of a "new liberal arts." By this I mean to signal a range of concerns from video literacy to modes of visual representations and the exciting new possibilities (enhanced by computer technology) of thinking interactively in visual terms (as opposed to one-way translation of our thoughts into visual representations).

To take up only the first e.g.: If it is true that 83 percent of American college students watch Saturday morning TV; if it is true that the average American spends seven-and-one-half hours a day in front of his or her video set, then it is the most urgent act of social responsibility for education to attend to this medium with all the kinds of attention and seriousness we have, hitherto, lavished on written texts. In the words of the recent AAC report, *Integrity in the College Curriculum*:

> Television is so much a part of our lives that it is foolish simply to deplore its weaknesses and bad habits. Students need to learn how to look at and listen to their television sets critically, with as much focused intellectual energy as they are expected to apply to other experiences that call upon their ability to listen and see intelligently.[6]

Television has become our national text, it holds pride of place in our nation's canon, it is the chief purveyor of worldviews and shaper of our lives as citizens. We cannot tolerate what my freshman class held almost unanimously last year, that the *New York Times* distorts the news (they have learned well the art of critical reading), but that television always shows you what actually happened. Walter Cronkite has won... "and that's the way it is." Among other consequences, the political implications of such naiveté are truly frightening.

I have sketched some exempli gratia that might suggest possibilities for experimentation towards a new frontier. You will have others; you will disagree with mine. What we celebrate as educators is, above all, acts of imagination in the sense stipulated by Wallace Stevens when he wrote, "Imagination is the power of the mind over the possibility of things." In the end, when all has been said, it is acts of imagination which must begin to shape the alternate present and the possible future for liberal education. The other option would be to await, yet again, endlessly and expectantly, the coming of last year.

Notes

"Towards Imagining New Frontiers," *Forum for Honors* 16 (Winter 1986). Pages 3–7 are reprinted by permission of the National Collegiate Honors Council.

1. Compare this opening passage with "Re-Forming the Undergraduate Curriculum," 100–101.—Ed.
2. William J. Bennett, *To Reclaim a Legacy: A Report on the Humanities in Higher Education* (Washington, DC: National Endowment for the Humanities, 1984). Cf. Smith, "Jonathan Z. Smith on William J. Bennett's 'To Reclaim

a Legacy: A Report on the Humanities in Higher Education,'" *American Journal of Education* 93, no. 4 (August 1985): 541–546.

3. On "liberal" and "servile" arts, see "Re-Forming the Undergraduate Curriculum," 94–96.—Ed.

4. On the SATs, see "Puzzlement," 129.—Ed.

5. On the importance to college work of argument and stakes, see "Puzzlement," 128–134.—Ed.

6. *Integrity in the College Curriculum: A Report to the Academic Community: The Findings and Recommendations of the Project on Redefining the Meaning and Purpose of Baccalaureate Degrees* (Washington, D.C.: Association of American Colleges, 1985), 17.

13

To Double Business Bound

AS A COLLEGE instructor, I have worried for years about the problems of teaching modes of active reading. One simple device I have used is to ask students to keep a journal-like set of notes in which they record their guesses, their questions, their comparisons between texts, and so forth, and to review these notes with them (along with the underlining in their texts) in individual conferences fairly early on in a course. I have just finished a 7:00 a.m. to 6:00 p.m. week of such meetings with students in my yearlong course on Religion in Western Civilization. In particular, I think of two students whose comments, made in passing, and taken together, would more than satiate any structuralist's lust for opposition and inversion. One was a student in the physical sciences; the other, a major in one of the social sciences.

The first student had his appointment with me shortly after a physics class. He complained that, contrary to his expectations, in the "hard sciences" (his term) nothing was definite. Matters he had laboriously mastered in high school were constantly being dismissed in college ("we no longer think that that is the case"), and he suspected that this would continue at each level of learning. He responded with depression to the same situation that Martin Gardner is said to have reported with enthusiasm some thirty years ago: A student at the Institute for Advanced Studies in Princeton was asked how his seminar had been that day. He was quoted as exclaiming, "Wonderful! Everything we knew about physics last week isn't true!" My student had come into my religion class in the belief that matters would be more certain there, that religion had secure knowledge. (He admitted that he found what we were doing in class just as depressing as his physics class.) The social sciences student had the opposite problem. As we reviewed her notebook together, she repeatedly insisted, "It's all bull." "Everything is interpretation." "You just deal with words, you have no facts." Both of these students are seniors. Both have been good students although not outstanding. Both are expecting to undertake post-baccalaureate studies.

If they appear to us to be naive—the physical science student with his odd nostalgia for the human sciences as the realm of unchanging truth and values, the social science student with her equally odd nostalgia for the physical sciences as a realm of fact and certainty—to whose account should this be charged? To the students'? Or to that of the education they have received? Neither student, despite the ten or twelve courses each has taken in his or her major program, has an adequate understanding of an academic discipline. The fault is surely ours, not theirs.

Interpretive Communities

At other times, and in other contexts, I might have used such an anecdote to introduce my long-standing suspicion of the major: that it is, at best, an inadequate mode of education given its stated goals; that it is, more usually, pernicious.[1] But that will not be my tack here. Rather, I will stipulate the presence of something like the major as a means of focusing education with its notion of "interpretive communities" or "knowledge communities," in order to raise some reformist or revisionist notions.

At the outset, we need to pause and be attentive to words. After all, the social science student was right. By and large, we academicians do deal with words. But rather than weakening us, as she thought, words are what empower us for good or ill—empower us with respect to the world, to other folk, and to one another within the academy. Anyone who doubts this need only turn to any number of works of feminist criticism, the most powerful and fundamental internal critique of the academy since Kant.

I like the terms *interpretive communities* or *discourse communities*. I think I like them even better than the word *disciplines*, which they are, in part, intended to replace. While *discipline* contains the notion of instruction and learning, it is the passive rather than the active sense that is to the fore, as its root *dek* (to accept) and the use of *discipline* as a transitive verb signify, and as its cognates *disciple, dogma,* and *docile* make plain. *Community* evokes a quite different politics. It carries the root connotation of exchange rather than subjugation. It suggests notions of common goods, reciprocity, and communication. Disciplines have students (that is, disciples); communities have colleagues. You can learn discipline; you must participate in a community.

Such lexicographical games are suggestive without necessarily having to bear the burden of being true. Indeed, when we look at a sophisticated definition of discipline, we find a far more social connotation than the word may, at first glance, seem to imply. The most thoughtful definition of discipline that I know appears in the first volume of Stephen Toulmin's masterwork, *Human Understanding*: "A collective human enterprise takes the form of a rationally developing 'discipline' in those cases where…[a] shared commitment to a sufficiently agreed set of ideals leads to the development of an isolable and self-defining repertory of procedures; and where those procedures are open to further modification so as to deal with problems arising from the incomplete fulfillment of those disciplinary ideals" (359). Note the central argument. For Toulmin, well-formed disciplines are constituted "not by the types of objects with which they deal [their subject matters], but rather by the questions which arise about them [their goals]" (149). The distinctive mark of a discipline is that these questions represent a shared commitment, a sufficient agreement, a collective enterprise (359). Disciplines are not given; they are not determined by what is out there. Rather, they are the result of a social compact, a covenant. It is their corporate "ideals" and goals—their projections rather than their achievements—that mark off disciplines from pseudo-disciplines and that distinguish one discipline from another.

This leads Toulmin to argue that continuity in a discipline is to be sought neither in the history of its so-called triumphs, its answers (the all-too-common banal and misleading mode of presenting the history of science), nor "in any single unchanging question or group of questions" (the equally common, banal, and misleading way of presenting the history of the human sciences, such as philosophy), but in what he terms the "continuing genealogy of problems" (148). Problems, as Toulmin understands them, are caused by the gap between a discipline's "ideals" and its "current capacities" (152). This gap generates "the isolable and self-defining repertory of procedures" characteristic of a given discipline. If I may be allowed, by way of an aside, to put this in my sort of language (with only rough congruence to Toulmin's), we choose a disciplinary stance—or perhaps more pointedly, at the subdisciplinary level, a theoretical or methodological posture—not by its successes so much as by the problems we are willing to live with. As a historian in the field of religion, I would rather go to bed at night with the headaches that position necessarily leads to than with the headaches entailed by the phenomenological approach of some of my colleagues. Because of the inescapable gap, disciplinary choice is as much, if not more, an index of pain than of pleasure.

Let's return to Toulmin. He uses a variety of languages to underscore the essentially social nature of his understanding of discipline. He writes that one must become an "heir" to the genealogy of problems (146, n.1). Elsewhere, he asserts that "the one indispensable step in any [disciplinary] apprenticeship" is "to enter imaginatively" into the discipline's "intellectual ideals" (153). At another point, he insists that there are "collective ambitions" one "commits" oneself to when one "enrolls" in the profession that corresponds to a given discipline (154). Finally, he affirms that a discipline is transmitted from one generation to another "by a process of enculturation" (159). Taken together, these sentences add up to an implicit theory and model of education.

I shall not tease out the lineaments of this model, for there is a rub. Toulmin's definition of discipline as I quoted it began with a limiting clause that I have thus far ignored: "a collective human enterprise takes the form of a rationally developing discipline in those cases..." (359). Elsewhere, Toulmin limits his definition by referring to "a compact discipline" (379). Such limiting terms will give neither aid nor comfort to anyone who would seek to identify the heterogeneous items that make up the present map of collegiate and curricular organization with Toulmin's understanding of discipline. The majority of motley subject areas that we politically recognize as fields or disciplines in our curricula fail at almost every point to fulfill Toulmin's definition of a "compact" and a "rationally developing" discipline. At best, they might be classified under the rubrics Toulmin develops towards the end of his work: "diffuse disciplines," "would-be disciplines," and "non-disciplinary intellectual activities" (378–411). In some instances, what our curricula do escapes even these generously flabby characterizations.

There is yet another issue. Toulmin's discussion requires that disciplines always be seen in relation to notions of professions and professionalism. To the degree that we continue to perceive liberal learning as distinct from preprofessional training (a distinction that is problematic), then the ethical question arises: Ought we to be engaged in enculturating college students into the several disciplines? Or, to put the matter more pragmatically: Should we continue to do the work of graduate education in college?[2] I would want to insist that, to either form of the question, the answer is no. It would be a separate argument to demonstrate that graduate education, more often than not, fails at achieving its legitimate educational goals, but that argument can be suggested by rephrasing the question: Why should college teachers continue to do worse at what graduate faculties already do badly?

Having looked briefly at the language of the disciplines, we need to return to the nomenclature *knowledge communities*, a suggestive term of uncertain pedigree. I confess that I was not helped much in thinking about the implications of this terminological shift by any number of readings, and therefore, I turn for clarification to the *gemeinschaft/gesellschaft* literature of social theory (with all its well-known problems) and, in particular, the classic work of Robert MacIver (1970). MacIver understood *community* to be a relative term. Nevertheless, he argued, it can be characterized "in some kind and degree [by] distinctive common characteristics—manners, traditions, modes of speech, and so on" (30). To this notion of community, he contrasted the *association*, which was "an organization of social beings (or a body of social beings as organized) for the pursuit of some common interest or interests. It is a determinate social unity built upon common purpose" (30). He went on to suggest that associations can be classified by their types of interests (for example, whether unspecialized or specialized) and the relative duration of their interests, from "temporary" and "realizable once for all" to "interests unlimited by a time-span" (56–59). I would add that associations, or organizations, are subgroups within a community (or can link subgroups across communities). While community usually implies singularity, organizations are more readily plural— a single individual can have simultaneous multiple memberships in a variety of organizations reflecting a plurality of interests. Finally, while communities strive for unity by encompassing diversity, organizations are frequently characterized by what anthropologists call segmentation. That is to say, when an organization reaches a certain, often demographic, limit, it splits. There is symmetrical balance and opposition between segments and unified resistance among all the segments to any superordinate entity.

I put this in terms of the present issue, and, mindful of a partial parallel to Toulmin's characterization of discipline, we might formulate matters in the following manner: the academy (as exemplified in a college or university) is a community; the several disciplines are organizations, usually oriented towards specialized goals of unlimited duration. Academic departments, which may or may not be coextensive with disciplines, serve as organizations that exhibit all the segmentary politics described by anthropologists: segmentation for largely demographic reasons, balanced opposition among themselves, and unitary resistance to a superordinate entity, usually the college or university as a whole.

Introductory Tasks

What have I gained by this sort of playful linguistic sleight of hand?[3] At the very least, it reminds us of something that the language of knowledge communities tempts us to fudge: there are two distinct introductory tasks that we confront as educators. The first is the introduction, the initiation, the enculturation of our students into the community of the college as different from the communities they know best, most particularly the world of home and of secondary schooling. The former we tend to address largely through the extra curriculum, ranging from residence (in some institutions) to diversity in admissions (in most). Curricularly, we address these issues only obliquely, by challenging students' notions of the authority of tradition, by instilling an ethic of everything, at least in principle, being open to suspicion and question. By largely confining the contrast between the college and home communities to the extracurricular, faculties have remained often unconscious of, indeed, blasé toward this most central, and often most painful, process of enculturation.

The students' second introduction, the initiation into the difference between the community of high school and that of college, especially with respect to work (a difference that, above all else, ought to be one of the most explicit objects of reflection in higher education) is chiefly seen as a matter of general education and, more recently, of programs in generic skills such as writing and critical reasoning. For central to this difference between communities is a change in attitude towards words and discourse. In college-level work, words are rarely thought to be expressive of things (in philosophical terms, they are no longer held to be "real"), they are no longer vocabularies to be mastered (*30 Minutes A Day*), or to be judged by the degree to which they conform to something "out there." In a college community, it is we who master words. Rather than evaluate the relationship of words to things, we evaluate the relationship of words to other words and to other acts of human imagination. It is a process that has many names; above all it is known as argumentation. For it is argument which marks the distinctive mode of speech which characterizes the college community.

There is latent in such a conception of the tasks of general education (when it is not reduced, in a core program or the like, to some notion of common acquaintance with a specific body of texts or concepts) a set of issues that have yet to be addressed widely by the educational community. Such matters have been raised in polemic works such as *Critical Thinking and Education* (McPeck 1981) as well as by some of the newer studies in rhetoric and by linguistic research in such fields as performance theory and pragmatics. Common to all these is suspicion of the notion of a universal audience and, therefore, a denial of the plausibility of generic argument and omnipurpose, omnicompetent writing capacities.

Disciplinary Barriers

To return to MacIver's characterizations, while it may be the case that the academy as a community can be distinguished from other communities by its modes of speech, the various organizations within the academy, because of their separate goals, may differ from one another even more widely. Allow me to quote three statements in illustration of this difference.

The first, taken from Gilbert Ryle's attack on the adequacy of universal notions of formal logic, points out that "a first-rate mathematician and a first-rate literary critic might share the one intellectual virtue of arguing impeccably, while their other intellectual virtues could be so disparate that neither could cope even puerilely with the problems of the other. Each thinks scrupulously inside his own field, but most of their scruples are of entirely different kinds" (1962, 21). The second statement is McPeck's bold assertion that "there are as many types of legitimate argument as there are fields or subjects that may be argued about.... And fields, with their corresponding modes of reasoning, differ more widely than species of animals" (1981, 79). While perhaps somewhat hyperbolic, his statement incarnates one of my old professors' definitions of a scholarly theory: "an exaggeration in the direction of the truth."

The third example is the most telling, for the author, the late Nobel Prize–winning physicist Richard Feynman, is innocent of any theoretical or educational purpose in reporting his anecdote. He writes that he decided to spend his summer vacations not by traveling to a different place but by studying in a different field. One summer and one sabbatical year were spent working on bacteriophages and doing other experiments in the biology laboratories at the California Institute of Technology. According to his report, his results were significant enough to interest

James Watson and to have Feynman himself invited to give a set of seminars to biologists at Harvard. Nevertheless, he says:

> [The] work on phage I never wrote up....I did write something informally on it. I sent it to [Bob] Edgar [who was in charge of the biology lab], who laughed when he read it. It wasn't in the standard form that biologists use—first, procedures, and so forth. I spent a lot of time explaining things that all the biologists knew. Edgar made a shortened version, but I couldn't understand it. I don't think they ever published it....I learned a lot of things in biology....I got better at pronouncing the words, knowing what not to include in a paper or a seminar, and detecting a weak technique in an experiment. But I love physics, and I love to go back to it. (Feynman 1985, 75–76)

Just how complex a matter Feynman signals with the phrase "it wasn't in the standard form that biologists use" may be illustrated by a number of careful studies, most especially the work of Knorr-Cetina (1981) that traces the development of a scientific research paper from the original experiment and lab notebook through all the intermediary draftings and revisions to the final published form.

Reflecting on these three examples produces any number of educational implications. The statements suggest, among other matters, that it may well be particular knowledge communities that ought to take chief responsibility for college-level writing, rather than programs in generic expository writing aimed at an abstract and universalized audience. Conversely, one might conclude that other modes of writing—especially more reflexive styles and genres, such as letters or journals—ought to be to the fore in general education courses as being particularly appropriate to these courses' task of enculturating the student into the academic community at large.

Feynman's anecdote allows us, as well, to begin to specify responsibilities implicit in the introductory role of the several knowledge communities, responsibilities that must gain explicit recognition in the communities' curricula, educational procedures, and objectives. Abstracting Feynman's themes, we can construct a rudimentary mini-curriculum for enculturating students into a given knowledge community. First, they need to learn something of the domain, or the topics, of the knowledge community, especially as expressed in the jargon of the field (compare Feynman's comment about getting "better at pronouncing the words"). Second, and even more important in many respects than becoming articulate in the field, is the contrary skill of mastering the repression of speech, learning the tacit conventions, the matters stipulated or taken for granted, which do not have to be said. (In Feynman's terms, the experience of "explaining things that all the biologists know.") Third, students must learn what counts as appropriate according to the conventions of the field (as Feynman learned how to detect "weak technique" and Ryle noted indigenous "scruples"). And fourth, students must become adept in the necessarily fictive modes of accepted disciplinary discourse. (This skill, suggested by Feynman's learning "what not to include in a paper or seminar," is raised to a procedural principle by the distinguished biologist Peter Medawar in his oft-cited observation that the conventions of the biological research paper not only "conceal but actively misrepresent" what occurs in the laboratory [1969, 69]).

Note the stunning results when these four tasks (and there are, of course, others) are not made an explicit part of a curriculum and an enculturation process. A Nobel laureate in physics is laughed at by his biologist colleagues when he writes up his biological experiments. Conversely, when a professional biologist writes up Feynman's experiments and results "in the standard form," Feynman cannot understand the result. How much more are such consequences compounded at the collegiate level, where the initiate is not a Nobel laureate but rather a neophyte or, God help us, a student from one knowledge community fulfilling a requirement in another community's course? By and large, it is only the first task, the "pronunciation of words," that is routinely and explicitly addressed. The other items, from which the faculty largely abstains, are left to the student's initiative (and failure), to his or her capacities for observation, for intuition, for mimesis—the same methods of learning, I would note, by which planaria become able to negotiate a maze.

Necessary Duplicities

It is at this point that we may fruitfully rejoin the two students with whom I began: the student in the physical sciences for whom surety gained at one stage of education was rudely overthrown at another, an individual who might be characterized as given to premature certainty, and the student in the social sciences for whom all was opinion and nothing secure, an individual who might be characterized as given to premature uncertainty.

Neither of these students had been let in on educators' pedagogical secret: the necessary duplicity of what educators do. Each saw one or the other side of educators' efforts, but we educators are to double business bound.

In introducing a college student to what is usually termed a disciplinary framework, we have, at first, to disguise the problematic. We have to act and speak as if our informed guesses are more grounded in the way things are than is the case. Thus every course, regardless of format, functions as a survey. It teaches the student what words are important and how to pronounce them. The words, the objects displayed, are taken as if they were self-evidently significant.[4] We conceal from our students the debates and uncertainties that lie behind such judgments—indeed, we largely conceal from them the fact that self-evidence is always a field-specific judgment. We traditionally screen from our students' view the hard work that results in the production of the exemplary texts, items, and problems on display—indeed, we treat these sources as found objects, hiding, for example, the immense editorial labors that conjecturally established so many of the texts routinely taken as classics (not to speak of the labors of translation), and read them with students as if each word were directly revelatory. In some courses, we also gloss over the history of failed experiments and sheer serendipity that underlies the laws and models we present to our students as inevitable. In enculturating courses, we treat theory as fact. Students in the humanities know that there is such a thing as an author's intention and regularly and effortlessly recover it. Students in the social sciences know that there is such a thing as a society that functions and regularly and effortlessly observe it. Students in the sciences are all (without knowing it) wedded to the philosophical tradition of induction that runs from Bacon to Mill and that, ironically, makes the students conceptually indistinguishable from Bible Belt creationists and fundamentalists.

Despite our claims to teach how and not what, as our students highlight their texts (call the texts in and look at them), it is the theoretical conclusions that they note with a yellow smear, not processes that do not lend themselves readily to such magic markings. And nothing we say or do in class, in assignments, or in examinations suggests that students should be otherwise engaged. In classroom discussion, as if at some afternoon television quiz show, they call out answers at one another and think they are discussing method.

The latter is reinforced by our laying on them the fake ethic of originality (one that is already inappropriate at the Ph.D. level and sheerly

ludicrous at the collegiate). In this way, we cover up the teamwork, col-
legiality, and interdependence that underlie most research activities, and
we leave students alone and separated from one another to cherish their
personal conclusions, often unconscious of how they reached them and
barred from making any procedural contrasts by means of examples,
interrogations, challenges, or rival proposals from their fellow students.
In a bizarre inversion, our structured forms of socialization into disciplinary communities result in onanism.

Second-Order Reflection

If, as I have suggested, all these concealments, all these acts of apparent
bad faith, are justified pedagogically by the strategic necessity for duplicity at the beginning, if we must behave in such a manner and encourage
our students to do likewise, then a dramaturge may properly ask, Where,
then, is the *peripeteia*? Where is the turnabout? Where is the unmasking?
At what point do we as teachers allow our students to experience what I
would call the wink? Is it at some point during a course? Is it along the
way of a four-year course of study? Is it a delayed payoff reserved only for
those who go on to postbaccalaureate study? I am more certain that these
sorts of questions are never asked by the majority of our faculties than I
am of the answers. I am quite certain that most students never experience
having the rug pulled out in a controlled way, never experience the gap
that Toulmin argued was at the very center of a definition of discipline. I
base this certainty on the fact that the curricula of most majors exhibit no
dramatic structure. When they are not sheerly political (that is, students
take a course with each professor), they are almost always constructed on
the principle of more-of-the-same.

If we intend to continue the use of something like the major as the
chief means of enculturation into a knowledge community in college,
then faculty discussions of sequences, prerequisites, requirements, and
certification will have to concern themselves largely with second-order
reflections and discourse about such disciplinary concerns and become
less preoccupied with first-order discourse concerning content. If faculty
discussions do not do this, dramatic duplicity will have shaded over into
fraud. Barring such discourse within the several organizations (that is,
the departments), each institution as a whole (the community) will have
to provide curricular time and space for students to reflect on their education in a way that the segmented faculty refuse to undertake. Either

way, we need to think hard about final moments—projects or occasions for students towards the end of their collegiate experiences—that are not merely more-of-the-same-only-longer but that provide a significant and, in some sense, public occasion for reflexivity.

Anthropologists employ the term *joking relationships* to describe a mode of social interaction between intimates. I would hope for no better model of the sort of dramatic, yet comfortable, relationship that ought to obtain between faculty and students, students and students, and faculty and students and their modes of disciplinary attention. Jokes, as any reader of Freud's masterwork will testify, are fundamentally untranslatable because they are always insiders' speech. Enculturation is achieved when the outsider becomes, to some degree, an insider.

It is time we let one another and, above all, it is time we let our students in on the joke, taking joke in the sense stipulated by a recent social theorist: "A joke is a play on form. It brings into relation disparate elements in such a way that one accepted pattern is challenged by another.... [The joke] affords the opportunity for realizing that an accepted pattern has no necessity" (Douglas 1968, 365). When all is said, disciplinary knowledge is this sort of joke and needs, for that very reason, to be taken seriously.

Notes

Carol Geary Schneider and William Scott Green, eds., *Strengthening the College Major*, New Directions for Higher Education, no. 84 [Winter 1993] (San Francisco: Jossey-Bass, 1993), 13–23. Reprinted by permission of John Wiley and Sons.

1. See "Why the College Major?" 111–118.—Ed.
2. On "liberal" (as opposed to "servile" arts), see "Re-Forming the Undergraduate Curriculum," 94–96.—Ed.
3. Compare the following pages with "Puzzlement," 124–128.—Ed.
4. On the temptation of self-evident significance, see also "Connections," 58–59.—Ed.

References

Douglas, Mary. 1968. "The Social Control of Cognition: Some Factors in Joke Perception." *Man* n.s., 3:361–376.

Feynman, Richard P. 1985. *"Surely You're Joking, Mr. Feynman."* New York: Norton.

Knorr-Cetina, Karin D. 1981. *The Manufacture of Knowledge: An Essay on the Constructivist and Contextual Nature of Science.* Elmsford, NY: Pergamon Press.

154   THE ACADEMIC PROFESSION

MacIver, Robert M. 1970. *On Community, Society and Power*. Chicago: University of Chicago Press.

McPeck, John E. 1981. *Critical Thinking and Education*. New York: St. Martin's Press.

Medawar, Peter B. 1969. *The Art of the Soluble*. New York: Viking Penguin.

Ryle, Gilbert. 1962. *A Rational Animal*. London: Athlone Press.

Toulmin, Stephen E. 1972. *Human Understanding*. Vol. 1. Princeton, NJ: Princeton University Press.

Editorial Remarks

Christopher I. Lehrich

WHEN I FIRST approached Jonathan Z. Smith about putting together this volume, I vaguely assumed that it would be part of my editorial task to provide some sort of commentary piece about the essays presented. However, when the time came to get down to brass tacks and work out details for the book, he was quite definite on the issue. "I've never allowed someone to introduce me that way," he said—and was kind enough to leave unspoken the corollary, "and I don't intend to start now."

For me, this is rather a blessing. Jonathan is a hard act to follow! But the anonymous readers unanimously demanded comment from me. In their reports, each indicated a small cluster of bits and pieces that they hoped I might provide, most significantly these:

1. How were these essays selected from the larger corpus?
2. What editorial work was done in the transcription?
3. What of the occasional nature of most of these pieces? In what context were they presented? to whom? and so forth.

Jonathan decided to deal with the latter point himself, in the form of the prefatory note he composed for this volume. The former two are the task of the present brief comment.

Selection

A near-complete bibliography of Smith's publications appears as an appendix to *Relating Religion*.[1] There one will find some thirty-odd essays that might, on the face of it, appear in a volume such as this.

I selected the present group on the basis of two general principles. First, I wanted pieces that stood well as essays in their own right, that is, in which the occasional nature of the work did not unduly dominate. Second, I wanted to avoid excessive repetition, a point about which Jonathan was also concerned.

For example, an obvious omission here is "Narratives into Problems."[2] That essay contains much which appears more extensively in the present volume, from the discussion of introductory religion courses in "The Introductory Course: Less Is Better" to the evaluation of disciplinary language and Richard Feynman's phage experiments in "To Double Business Bound." Additionally, since "Narratives into Problems" is immediately accessible to religion scholars via JSTOR, it seemed appropriate to exclude.

Many of us have favorite J. Z. teaching essays, and inevitably some do not appear here. In a few cases, Jonathan expressed a strong preference for this essay over that, or flatly rejected an essay's inclusion, and I have of course respected his wishes. On the whole, though, we were in agreement about which essays worked best when combined into a single volume.

Editorial Work

All told, my editorial labors were not especially onerous when it came to the texts. The principal issues concerned citations and cross-references.

Bearing in mind that most of these essays were originally lectures, and that the citation practices of the journals and volumes varied considerably, it is no surprise that the reference styles were inconsistent. Where possible, I simply regularized the formats, but in some cases more was required. My aim throughout has been to preserve the style of the original, keeping editorial manipulation to a minimum while establishing a relatively consistent final text. For example, with "To Double Business Bound," I found that I could not shift all the references to endnotes without dramatically altering the prose style, so I left it with parenthetical in-text references and standardized their format and the bibliography.

As to cross-references, the question was practical utility. I expect that many of these essays will be excerpted and read by groups—in faculty meetings, graduate pedagogy workshops, and curricular-planning discussions. For such a readership, it is essential to have each essay stand on its own. Yet I hope that many will wish to follow up, to look at what else the author said on an issue, or where else he used similar examples and comments. At the same time, I have tried not simply to construct a second running index, nor to insert any covert editorial commentary.

The cross-references are intended as a means of ensuring maximum utility with a minimum of interference. I was consoled in this time-consuming and frustrating task by knowing that Jonathan had suffered much the same problem, on an enormously greater scale, when editing the *HarperCollins Dictionary of Religion* (see "Connections," 51–52).

Beyond this, I tried to keep my editorial hand as light as possible. For example, I made no square-bracket insertions in the main text: all such insertions are Smith's, though in a few clearly indicated places I have made an editorial insertion in a note. All ellipses are Smith's. Minor formatting changes, spelling and punctuation corrections, and the like were made silently. In a few instances where changes had been made by previous editors, Smith's original texts have been silently reintroduced.

It remains only to thank the many friends and colleagues who have supported this work, and, most of all, to thank Jonathan for permitting me to pursue it.

Notes

1. Appendix, *Relating Religion: Essays in the Study of Religion* (Chicago: University of Chicago Press, 2004), 391–402.
2. "'Narratives into Problems': The College Introductory Course and the Study of Religion," *Journal of the American Academy of Religion* 56, no. 4 (Winter 1988): 727–739.

Index